The Dangers of Hallucinogens

Jenny MacKay

ReferencePoint Press®

San Diego, CA

© 2017 ReferencePoint Press, Inc.
Printed in the United States

For more information, contact:
ReferencePoint Press, Inc.
PO Box 27779
San Diego, CA 92198
www. ReferencePointPress.com

LIBRARY OF CONGRESS CATALOGING-IN-PUBLICATION DATA

Names: MacKay, Jenny, 1978- author.
Title: The dangers of hallucinogens / by Jenny MacKay.
Description: San Diego, CA : ReferencePoint Press, Inc., 2017. | Series: Drug
dangers | Includes bibliographical references and index.
Identifiers: LCCN 2015048354 (print) | LCCN 2016005207 (ebook) | ISBN
9781682820162 (hardback) | ISBN 9781682820179 (epub)
Subjects: LCSH: Hallucinogenic drugs--Juvenile literature. | Drug
abuse--Juvenile literature.
Classification: LCC HV5822.H25 M23 2017 (print) | LCC HV5822.H25 (ebook) |
DDC 362.29/4--dc23
LC record available at http://lccn.loc.gov/2015048354

CONTENTS

Chapter 1   **4**
Hallucinogens: The Scope of the Problem

Chapter 2   **17**
Effects of Using Hallucinogens

Chapter 3   **30**
Hallucinogens and the Potential for Addiction

Chapter 4   **41**
Challenges in Treating Hallucinogen Use

Chapter 5   **53**
Preventing the Abuse of Hallucinogens

Source Notes   **65**

Organizations to Contact   **69**

For Further Research   **73**

Index   **75**

Picture Credits   **79**

About the Author   **80**

CHAPTER 1: Hallucinogens: The Scope of the Problem

Plants have played crucial roles in people's lives over the course of human history. Trees, shrubs, and grasses have historically been used around the world to build shelters, for example, and plants have always been a major source of food. Early humans were gatherers and foragers, sampling plants and other things that grew in the world around them (including fungi such as molds and mushrooms) to find options that were edible. These foraging activities involved risk, since not all things that grew were safe to ingest. Certain kinds of plants and many fungi were poisonous, causing illness and even death.

A few types of plants and fungi seemed to have healing properties, however, and in time some came to be used as medicine. Still other plants and fungi produced strange effects on the minds of people who consumed them, altering their thoughts and emotions and especially the way their senses interpreted their environment. All around the earth, people began ingesting such substances for exactly this reason. Many such plants and fungi became an important part of religious ceremonies or social rituals in societies around the world.

Substances that cause a person to feel disconnected from reality are known today as hallucinogens. Scientists and health professionals have learned that many risks can accompany their use. In addition to causing strange and sometimes dangerous behavior, some of these substances can do serious and permanent damage to a person's brain, making such drugs targets for legal and public regulation despite their popular use by people seeking to experience often unpredictable mental effects.

From Nature to Laboratories

Since ancient times, people have known of the potency of various hallucinogenic plants. Early Mesoamerican peoples and North African tribes left visual records of their experimentation with mushrooms; archaeological digs reveal that indigenous peoples of the Americas have used peyote cacti and other plants since prehistoric times to induce hallucinogenic states in healing rituals and other spiritual ceremonies. Western Europeans who encountered indigenous tribes in the Americas during the sixteenth century were initially shocked by the drug-induced behaviors they witnessed in these rituals. Missionaries interpreted the drug-induced states as signs of Satan's power over the pagans. However, colonials quickly realized that the hallucinogens played a significant role in tribal medicine, and some early European naturalists began to catalog the plants and their effects.

The peyote cactus (pictured) is a powerful hallucinogen that has been used by North American indigenous peoples since prehistoric times as part of healing rituals and other spiritual ceremonies.

By the late 1800s and early 1900s, European scientists had learned how to produce certain plant and fungal chemicals in laboratories. In 1888, for example, German toxicologist Louis Lewin distilled the hallucinogenic alkaloids in peyote, determining that mescaline was the most potent of its psychotropic compounds. In 1919 Austrian chemist Ernst Späth synthesized mescaline in his laboratory. In 1938 Swiss chemist Albert Hofmann reacted a weak alkaline—diethylamine—with lysergic acid derived from a grain fungus. Doing so produced lysergic acid diethylamide (commonly abbreviated as LSD). This chemical produced strange behavior in rats but was otherwise uninteresting to most scientists. Hofmann, however, was unable to forget about it. In 1943 he accidentally absorbed some of the drug through his fingers as he was handling it. He experienced a variety of strange effects, including dizziness, a strange desire to laugh, and weird changes in the way he saw things.

> "My surroundings had now transformed themselves in more terrifying ways. Everything in the room spun around, and the familiar objects and pieces of furniture assumed grotesque, threatening forms."[1]
>
> —Chemist Albert Hofmann.

When he intentionally ingested the LSD again a few days later, Hofmann's experiences were even stranger and more intense. He later wrote of his experiences in his laboratory journal:

> Everything in my field of vision wavered and was distorted as if seen in a curved mirror. . . . My surroundings had now transformed themselves in more terrifying ways. Everything in the room spun around, and the familiar objects and pieces of furniture assumed grotesque, threatening forms. They were in continuous motion, animated, as if driven by an inner restlessness. The lady next door, whom I scarcely recognized, brought me milk. . . . She was no longer Mrs. R., but rather a malevolent, insidious witch with a colored mask.[1]

Street Names of Hallucinogens

Like many illegal substances people use to get high, hallucinogens often have nicknames. Different drugs have different effects on the body, and it is helpful for police officers, health care workers, and others to know a drug's nicknames so they can identify what someone might have used or what is being sold or offered. Popular nicknames for common hallucinogens include the following:

- Lysergic acid diethylamide (LSD): acid, blotter, California sunshine or yellow sunshine, Lucy in the Sky with Diamonds, Loony Toons (LSD is often produced on small squares of paper printed with cartoon images, giving it many names), Superman, microdots (tiny, ball-shaped pills)

- Phencyclidine (PCP): angel dust, wack, cliffhanger, happy sticks, Peter Pan, lethal weapon, peace pill

- Mushrooms: magic mushrooms, shrooms, magics, blue meanies, liberty caps, golden tops, mushies

- Ketamine: K, special K, jet, super acid, green

- Methylenedioxymethamphetamine (MDMA): ecstasy, Molly, MD, M, E, XTC, love drug

- Cannabis: marijuana, pot, dope, weed, grass, reefer, Mary Jane, hashish

As their often quirky-sounding names may imply, hallucinogens cause a variety of emotional, physical, and mental changes in users and alter a person's ability to make logical decisions or do things like drive a vehicle safely. Beneath the lighthearted nicknames lie drugs whose effects can be unpredictable and even dangerous—especially if users are unclear from the name exactly what substance they are being offered.

When Hofmann recovered from these strange effects, he realized he had created a drug that produced powerful hallucinations. LSD was thus the first hallucinogen synthesized in a laboratory setting.

Through the 1940s, 1950s, and 1960s, scientists—especially psychiatrists—began to give LSD to patients to see what effects it had on psychosis, a mental disorder that causes a disconnection from reality. The scientists found no medical uses for LSD and therefore did not recommend it as a treatment. Meanwhile, however, the laboratory that manufactured the drug—Sandoz Pharmaceuticals—had begun making and distributing free samples of LSD, which found their way into the hands of everyday users.

By the 1960s LSD had become a popular street drug, but its powerful and varied effects concerned government authorities. In the United States the sometimes psychotic episodes of users convinced states to ban LSD; the first state to do so was California in 1966. However, LSD's underground popularity did not diminish, especially in a decade of youth rebellion and the questioning of traditional belief systems. Some young people, for example, continued to experiment with "acid" in an effort to experience spiritual, sensual, and interpersonal insights. This marked a shift in the use of hallucinogens around the world. People no longer relied on plants and fungi they knew caused strange mental effects. They now could manufacture such substances in forms that could be swallowed, smoked, and even injected.

Since the 1960s LSD and related lysergamides have been manufactured in a variety of forms. Small pills or tablets are the most typical, but LSD can also be applied to small squares of blotting paper, sugar cubes, or even squares of gelatin (like Jell-O) that are eaten. It can also come in liquid form, usually stored in a small vial. LSD has been applied to colorful squares of paper printed with images of rainbows or happy faces. These may give the user the impression that the drug is fun and harmless, but in fact, LSD and other lysergamides have produced physical changes such as elevated heart rate, tremors, and numbness, as well as mental distortions that can lead to panic attacks, paranoia, or psychosis.

Types of Hallucinogens

Modern-day hallucinogens are not limited to lysergamides. However, like lysergamides, the diversity of hallucinogens can be grouped by their shared chemical structures. One group, called piperidines, are drugs made from a peppery-smelling liquid by the same name. Phencyclidine, commonly known as PCP, is a common piperidine. It was developed in the 1950s as an anesthetic, a drug that, when taken in low doses, reduces or eliminates the sensation of pain. However, doctors became alarmed by the strange effects PCP had on many patients. Even if the dosage was controlled, PCP could cause unpredictable mood swings and other changes in behavior. Pharmacologists Steven B. Karch and Olaf Drummer say, "Human use of PCP was discontinued after it was discovered that 10%–20% of patients given PCP became delirious and/or unmanageable for many hours after surgery." Americans began to make, sell, and use the substance illegally as a street drug in the 1960s. According to Karch and Drummer, "The drug rapidly developed a reputation for causing antisocial, violent behavior."[2] In unregulated doses, the drug may foster paranoia and even prompt suicidal thoughts in users.

Another piperidine is ketamine, an anesthetic that veterinarians typically use on animals. Ketamine dulls pain sensations but can also make the user feel sluggish and have difficulty moving. Both PCP and ketamine can be produced as pills that can be swallowed or as powder that can be dissolved in liquid. Some people use a syringe to inject the drug into a vein. Piperidines in liquid or powder form can also be applied to leaves of plants, such as marijuana leaves, and smoked. Although used less commonly than LSD, piperidines are strong hallucinogens and can affect their users in unpredictable and sometimes dangerous ways.

Often used with piperidines like PCP, marijuana is itself a hallucinogen. It comes from the hemp plant, whose leaves, stems, and flowers are typically dried and then smoked (although they

> "Human use of PCP was discontinued after it was discovered that 10%–20% of patients given PCP became delirious and/or unmanageable for many hours after surgery. . . . The drug rapidly developed a reputation for causing antisocial, violent behavior."[2]
>
> —Pharmacologists Steven B. Karch and Olaf Drummer.

can also be eaten and are sometimes added to brownies or other baked goods). Marijuana belongs to a third type of hallucinogenic (hallucination-causing) drugs known as cannabinoids. Its effects on the brain and the behavior of those who use it are usually more predictable and less dangerous than the effects of stronger hallucinogens like PCP. Cannabinoids typically produce a sense of euphoria, but some of the hallucinatory effects can lead to anxiety. When PCP and marijuana are combined and smoked, the euphoric effects of the marijuana are more intense and longer lasting, while the dissociative effects of the PCP are also heightened. The combination can be especially unpredictable when users are not aware that a second hallucinogen such as PCP has been applied to the marijuana.

A fourth class of hallucinogens is the indolealkylamines, whose chemicals are found in certain kinds of mushrooms. People use mushrooms by swallowing them, sometimes when they

Most frequently ingested through smoking, as seen in this photo, marijuana is the hallucinogenic form of the hemp plant. Though marijuana's hallucinogenic effects are relatively mild, they can be more intense and dangerous when the drug is combined with a stronger hallucinogen such as PCP.

are fresh but more commonly after they are dried, cooked, or frozen. Mushrooms can also be ground into a powder or made into pills or capsules. One of the main dangers of mushrooms is that many varieties are poisonous, and these can be difficult to tell apart from the types that cause hallucinations. People have gotten sick and even died from confusing one type of mushroom with another.

Substances called phenylethylamines make up the fifth major class of hallucinogens. Phenylethylamines are alkaloids common in plant life and even in mammals. In humans these alkaloids occur in the nervous system, boosting a person's feelings of happiness and affection for other people. Phenylethylamines in the form of mescaline occur naturally in the peyote cactus and have been used to stimulate feelings of excitement and induce hallucinations. Some variants have been synthesized in laboratories to produce amphetamines and methamphetamines that mimic these effects.

More recently, methylenedioxymethamphetamine, or MDMA, has become a popular street drug. Known as ecstasy, the drug became widely used at dance parties called raves. Usually taken in pill form, it causes hallucinations and also enhances feelings of love, energy, and excitement that seem to correlate with the crowded dance floor experience. Like all classes of hallucinogens, phenylethylamines like ecstasy can have unpredictable and unwanted effects—such as confusion, depression, dehydration, and anxiety—in the people who use them.

How Hallucinogens Work

Hallucinogens come from many sources and occur in many types and forms, but they share one thing in common—they have mysterious effects on their users. These effects are often very different, depending on the type of hallucinogen and the person who is using it. Even stranger, the same hallucinogen taken by the same person can cause entirely different effects each time it is used. Research has shown that hallucinogens work by tweaking the normal function of the brain, the body's most complex and least understood organ. The mysterious and unpredictable nature of hallucinogens makes them difficult for scientists to understand, and they are therefore also potentially dangerous for people to use.

The brain contains a complicated system of nerve cells that pass small charges of electrical energy from one to the next at lightning speed. These electrical pulses carry messages between the brain and the body. The body produces chemicals called neurotransmitters to help brain cells communicate with each other; neurotransmitters ensure that these electrical messages get sent to the right places in the brain or body. Brain cells have special receptors—like tiny docking stations—where neurotransmitters attach. Neurotransmitters work like switches, turning brain cells on or off to help electrical messages travel along the proper pathways to reach their destination.

Hallucinogens primarily attach to a receptor for serotonin, a neurotransmitter that helps influence mood and well-being. The chemicals in hallucinogens bind to the receptor and excite it, sending signals that otherwise might not be sent. The brain will struggle to make sense of these phantom messages, and it might send out the wrong instructions for what the body is supposed to do in response. Thus, chemicals in hallucinogens alter perception of what a person actually sees, hears, tastes, smells, or feels. In return, the brain instructs the body to react to what is basically a false situation. To an observer, someone under the influence of hallucinogens will act irrationally or refer to sights, sounds, or smells that are not real. One person who posted to the Experience Project website described an acid trip after taking LSD-laden pills. The user reported he hallucinated that an insect crawled into his ear. In an attempt to get it out, he asked a friend to peek into his ear. "He was trying to look while I was shaking my head about completely disturbed (I could still hear it moving!)," the user said. "He was telling me relax, it is the acid messing with your mind, but [in] my head I KNEW there was something in my ear."[3]

"I was shaking my head about completely disturbed . . . He was telling me relax, it is the acid messing with your mind, but [in] my head I KNEW there was something in my ear."[3]

—Annonymous LSD user.

The CIA's History with LSD

When LSD was found to cause users to experience a separation from reality, the CIA became interested in knowing more about the drug and its effects. From 1954 to 1963 in the cities of San Francisco and New York, the CIA carried out project MK-ULTRA, which involved conducting LSD experiments on members of the public without their knowledge. CIA agents would slip the drug to unsuspecting users in a variety of situations and follow them to see how they behaved under its influence. They learned, among other things, that a user's mood and the setting in which the drug is taken contribute to the kind of experience the user will have. If he or she is in a positive mood and a friendly setting, the experience is more likely to be uplifting, whereas if the user is fearful, angry, or in distress, the experience is more likely to be frightening or depressing.

Administering drugs to people without their knowledge is unethical, and when the CIA's program was brought to light, it shook Americans' trust in their government. After the agency ended its experiments in 1964, the US government decided LSD was too dangerous for the general public and made it illegal to use or sell. This chapter in the history of LSD shows some of the influence the substance has had on the minds and even the policies of Americans, sometimes without their knowledge.

The effects of tweaked brain messages can seem mystical, fascinating, and even funny to a person who has taken a hallucinogen, but the brain's method of sending messages is delicate and complicated. Tinkering with this process is risky. Usually, the effects of hallucinogens eventually wear off and the brain returns to normal, but this could take anywhere from hours to days. The time it takes to recover from using hallucinogens varies widely from drug to drug, person to person, and even from use to use of the same drug by the same person.

An Illegal Class of Drugs

The effects of hallucinogens are unpredictable, and these drugs have the potential to forever alter someone's brain. They also have no known medical benefits, despite the fact that some cultures have used them in healing rituals. This information has led the US government to classify most hallucinogens as Schedule I drugs under the Controlled Substances Act. This means they fall into the most dangerous out of five classes of drugs, a status they share with other harmful drugs such as heroin. Schedule I substances are considered to have "a high potential for abuse and potentially severe psychological and/or physical dependence,"[4] according to the Drug Enforcement Administration.

LSD, mushrooms, peyote, and MDMA (ecstasy) are classified as Schedule I drugs. PCP is a Schedule II drug because it is still a viable anesthetic (chiefly used in veterinarian medicine). Of all these hallucinogens, only peyote is given a special exemption from legal prosecution if it is used as part of Native American religious rituals. In all other cases, making, selling, or possessing peyote or any of the rest of these drugs brings stiff judicial sentences, which typically include jail time.

Hallucinogen Use in the United States

Criminalizing the use of hallucinogens, however, has not stopped their use. According to the Substance Abuse and Mental Health Services Administration's 2014 National Survey on Drug Use and Health, 936,000 people aged twelve and up tried hallucinogens for the first time during the previous twelve-month period, and 1.2 million Americans (or 0.4 percent of the population) reported using hallucinogens at some time in their lives. That number has remained fairly consistent since 2002. Of all hallucinogen use, the use of ecstasy accounted for half of that figure (609,000 persons aged twelve and up).

Of the 1.2 million hallucinogen users, 136,000 were aged twelve to seventeen (or 0.5 percent of the adolescent population). In that twelve-to-seventeen age range, 65,000 had used LSD, and 39,000 had used ecstasy. The National Institute on Drug Abuse reports that between 2002 and 2008, the use of ecstasy was more prevalent in girls aged twelve to seventeen than in boys of the same age. More recent research from Joseph J. Palamar and Dimitra Kamboukos of NYU Langone Medical Center's De-

Young Adults Comprise Largest Percentage of Hallucinogen Users

According to the 2014 National Survey on Drug Use and Health, young adults between the ages of eighteen and twenty-five make up the largest percentage of hallucinogen users in the United States. This finding has been consistent dating back to 2002. The survey shows that 1.4 percent of people in this age group used hallucinogens in 2014. Adolescents between the ages of twelve and seventeen represented the next largest percentage of hallucinogen users, at 0.5 percent in 2014. People aged twenty-six or older represented the final group, at 0.3 percent. The survey notes that the total hallucinogen user population in the United States in 2014 was an estimated 1.2 million people.

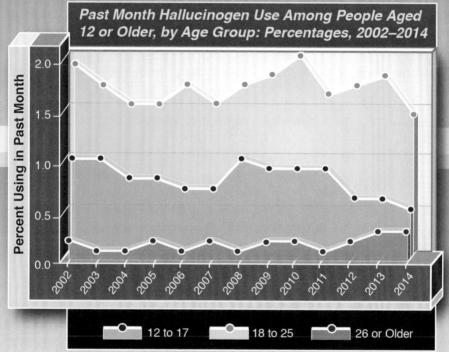

Past Month Hallucinogen Use Among People Aged 12 or Older, by Age Group: Percentages, 2002–2014

12 to 17   18 to 25   26 or Older

Source: Sarra L. Hedden et al., "Behavioral Health Trends in the United States: Results from the 2014 National Survey on Drug Use and Health," SAMHSA, September 2015. www.samhsa.gov.

partment of Population Health found that high school senior girls were at less risk for ecstasy use but that the use of tobacco, alcohol, or illicit drugs markedly increased the chance that both male and female high school seniors would use ecstasy.

Although trends in usage have remained stable, the government and law enforcement officials still consider LSD, ecstasy, and other hallucinogens to be very dangerous. The legal consequences for making, possessing, or using hallucinogens are serious and may include fines and jail time. However, the worst risks and dangers of using hallucinogens come from the effects of these substances on the body, especially the brain. Doctors and scientists still do not fully understand how hallucinogens work to alter brain function, and they have found no way to predict exactly what effect these drugs might have on a person's behavior. Therefore, people who use hallucinogens take great risks with their health and well-being, potentially causing damage to their brain that can never be fixed or reversed.

CHAPTER 2: Effects of Using Hallucinogens

Hallucinogens change how things look, sound, smell, taste, and feel. While under their influence, people perceive things very differently. Sometimes their experiences inspire awe, wonder, and feelings of love and affection. Other times people are overcome by fear, paranoia, sadness, and even terror. Such changes to a person's mental state are completely unpredictable, however, and do not always wear off and disappear, as the user might expect.

A Trip Through Distorted Reality

Different hallucinogens have various effects on the brain and nervous system. Many of them, including LSD, mushrooms, and peyote, have psychedelic effects. This means they change the brain's normal thoughts and methods for making sense of touch, sights, sounds, smells, and tastes. The word *psychedelic* comes from two Greek words that loosely mean "mind revealing." Under the influence of psychedelic drugs, individuals usually perceive things that are not real. They might see colorful patterns or swirls moving around on walls or in the sky, for example, or strange objects like polka-dotted elephants or dancing flowers. Hallucinations can involve the other senses, too. Users might believe they can smell or taste colors, hear sounds from the imaginary things they see, or touch visual hallucinations with their hands.

Some hallucinations can seem happy or funny, but others are not enjoyable at all. People having what is known as a "bad trip" often feel trapped in a vivid nightmare. Their brain might be tricked into perceiving that they are covered in spiders or snakes, that monsters are chasing them, or that they are on fire. People who use hallucinogens might genuinely believe they feel pain even when there is no physical basis for it. "For some people,

Although some drugs can produce pleasant or amusing hallucinations, someone having a bad trip may experience nightmarish sensations such as being covered in or surrounded by snakes or spiders. This can lead to feelings of severe panic.

the psychedelic experience may be frightening or terrifying," say toxicologists Frank F. Daly and Luke Yip. Common symptoms of a bad trip, they say, are "acute panic reactions" combined with "anxiety, apprehension, a sense of loss of self-control, and frightening illusions."[5]

Whether good or bad, psychedelic trips typically last a few hours to a day or even longer. Frequent users may plan for some of the effects to last through an extended weekend of three or four days. Even though their experiences are caused entirely by the drug, the interference with the brain's normal functioning often makes it impossible for the person to tell the difference between what is real and what is not. There is also no way to predict whether a trip will be a bad one. "Hallucinogenic drug effects may be variable, even in the same individual on different occasions,"[6] say Daly and Yip. Upon any given use of a hallucinogen, a person risks getting stuck for hours in a terrifying imaginary world he or she cannot escape.

Dissociating from Reality

Other hallucinogens are known as dissociatives. To dissociate means to disconnect or separate; these drugs, which include ketamine and PCP, affect the user's brain in a way that makes him or her feel separate or detached from the environment and even his or her own body. Users of these drugs might believe they are having visions of a higher power or are receiving spiritual knowledge. Hallucinations may simply change behavior and compel users to act in very dangerous ways. One Connecticut woman called local police after her boyfriend, who had a history of PCP use, accused her of being the devil. She told officers that he had run out of the house naked with her baby and appeared to be under the influence of drugs. A reporter for the *Hartford Courant* explains where the man was discovered: "An I-95 on-ramp. When the cops came to arrest him, he was sitting naked on the roadway, after having passed the baby off on a random motorist who stopped to render assistance. (The baby was not hurt.)"[7]

> "For some people, the psychedelic experience may be frightening or terrifying."[5]
>
> —Toxicologists Frank F. Daly and Luke Yip.

To users of PCP or other dissociatives, sights and sounds seem distorted, and users may feel as if they are floating. Dissociative drugs also affect users' perception of space and time. Individuals may become unaware of how many minutes or hours have passed, for example, and might lose the ability to estimate the distance between themselves and the traffic in the street or the distance to the ground if they climb on something. Such changes to perception can cause users not to recognize dangers in everyday situations.

Dissociative hallucinogens often cause users to develop false beliefs about the body's abilities, too. People who have taken such a substance might believe they have superhuman strength or are able to fly. One contributor to the Erowid website states that after smoking PCP, "I felt like going outside and picking a fight. I felt invincible."[8] Dissociative drugs like PCP also have anesthetic effects, meaning they cause numbness and reduce the ability to feel pain. Users are therefore at risk of hurting themselves or other people because they might believe they are invincible, and nothing seems painful to them. "There is nothing about PCP that suddenly increases an individual's muscle mass or improves muscle function," says psychiatrist Terry Rustin. "Rather, intoxicated individuals do not believe they can be hurt and have no inhibitions, so they attack suddenly and with 100% of their strength."[9] When the effects of the drug wear off, however, users will feel pain from any injuries that occurred.

Effects on Personality and Behavior

Hallucinogens cause behavior changes as well. A normally functioning brain processes details from one's surroundings and provides information about what to do next. Social skills depend on this ability. People know, for example, that it is acceptable to shout and cheer if they are watching a baseball game but not if they are attending a funeral. Such restrictions on behavior are called *social inhibitions*. People learn to avoid certain behaviors when they do not want to be offensive or impolite or if they do not know another person very well.

A person whose behavior is altered by hallucinogens, however, may lose the ability to correctly interpret social scenarios. Hallucinogens can completely erase social inhibitions until the drug's effects wear off, which can put people at risk of dangerous behaviors they would not normally undertake. For example, many hallucinogens boost a person's feelings of affection for others while masking the inhibitions that might normally prevent promiscuous behavior—sexual acts in which a person participates without considering consequences or even knowing the other person.

> "There is nothing about PCP that suddenly increases an individual's muscle mass or improves muscle function. Rather, intoxicated individuals do not believe they can be hurt and have no inhibitions, so they attack suddenly and with 100% of their strength."[9]
>
> —Psychiatrist Terry Rustin.

Hallucinogens Are Hard on Teeth

The club drug ecstasy is notoriously risky for people's bodies—right down to their teeth. Using ecstasy can tense muscles, including those of the jaw. Ecstasy users sometimes clench their jaws and grind their teeth for hours on end every time they use the drug. Studies have shown that frequent ecstasy users can actually grind through their tooth enamel—the substance that protects the soft tissue and the nerves inside the tooth. When this happens, the tooth's root can become exposed, which is very painful. People are also far more likely to suffer from tooth infections, decay, missing or broken teeth, and other serious dental problems if they grind the enamel off their teeth.

Other hallucinogens, including marijuana, can also contribute to chronic dry mouth. The absence of saliva not only causes bad breath but can lead to rapid tooth decay. Such problems might seem minor at the time, but they could set in motion a series of dental problems that will last a user's entire life.

Ashley, who first tried ecstasy when she was twelve, told her story to PBS: "You're feeling good, so you'll do whatever makes you happy for the moment. And the next day you sit down, and you think about it, and you're like, 'Oh my God . . . I had unprotected sex with this guy.' . . . I don't know how many girls he's ever been with, what if I got something. I was in that situation and had to go get HIV tested."[10]

Hallucinogen use can lead to other strange behavior that is out of character for users. If people believe they are surrounded by terrifying things, they may panic and become violent in an effort to protect themselves or escape. Individuals under the influence might also become convinced that people are out to get them and might frighten or hurt innocent bystanders who they mistakenly believe are a danger or a threat. They might break a window and try to climb through the broken glass, run across a busy street, leap out of a moving car, or fling themselves off the balcony of a building. This is what happened to Tyrone Lee Underwood, a forty-one-year-old Texan who jumped from a four-story hotel window in October 2008. According to a woman present in the hotel room, Underwood was acting irrationally, pounding on the walls and shouting "Yes, Lord, yes, Lord"[11] before breaking through the glass. An autopsy showed traces of PCP in his body.

It is not always possible to reason with or calm someone who has taken hallucinogens and become violent, and a person in this state has the potential to seriously harm other people. If police officers are called to the scene, they may be in danger as well. It can be very difficult to restrain a person who has used a halluci-nogen. Police sometimes resort to spraying tear gas or mace (a spice-based spray used for self-defense) in the face of a violent offender. However, some hallucinogenic drugs, especially PCP, can mask discomfort and make tear gas or mace ineffective. If police officers are unaware that a person has used a hallucino-gen, they may be surprised when attempts to calm him or her do not work. "People under the influence of PCP appear to be im-pervious to pain and require many officers to successfully subdue them,"[12] says law enforcement expert Chuck Joyner.

In addition to altering a person's perceptions, hallucinogens can also cause rapid and wild mood swings, ranging from joyful giggling to overwhelming despair. When the brain is impaired by a hallucinogen, it is incapable of reasoning normally. Therefore, the person does not realize and cannot be convinced that the pow-erful emotions are temporary and will likely cease once the drug wears off. A user of these drugs might even feel so overcome with depression that he or she attempts suicide. The potential of hallucinogens to cause severe despair, panic, and anxiety can be very dangerous for people if it makes them feel like harming or killing themselves.

Long-Term or Permanent Effects

Because scientists believe hallucinogens affect neurotransmitters' ability to function properly, they fear that damage may become permanent, altering the way sensory messages move properly from one nerve cell to the next. That is, once this process has been altered with a hallucinogen, it might not work exactly the

Short-Term and Long-Term Effects of Hallucinogens

Hallucinogen use can result in both short-term and long-term effects involving the senses, the physical body, and the mental and emotional state of the user. Some of the most common perception-altering effects of hallucinogens take place in the prefrontal cortex of the brain. This part of the brain is involved in mood, cognition, and perception. Hallucinogens also affect areas of the brain that regulate arousal and physiological responses to stress and panic.

Short-Term Effects

Sensory Effects

- Hallucinations (including seeing, hearing, touching, or smelling things in a distorted way or perceiving things that do not exist)

- Intensified feelings and sensory experiences (brighter colors, sharper sounds)

- Mixed senses ("seeing" sounds or "hearing" colors)

- Changes in sense or perception of time (time goes by slowly)

Physical Effects

- Increased energy and heart rate
- Nausea

Long-Term Effects

Persistent psychosis

- Visual disturbances
- Disorganized thinking
- Paranoia
- Mood disturbances

Hallucinogen Persisting Perception Disorder (HPPD)

- Hallucinations
- Other visual disturbances (such as seeing halos or trails attached to moving objects)

Symptoms sometimes mistaken for neurological disorders (such as stroke or brain tumor)

Source: National Institute on Drug Abuse, "How Do Hallucinogens (LSD, Psilocybin, Peyote, DMT, and Ayahuasca) Affect the Brain and Body?," National Institutes of Health, February 2015. www.drugabuse.gov.

same as before. Thus, while most hallucinogen-induced effects are temporary, these drugs can also have long-term or permanent effects.

Days, weeks, months, or even years after using a hallucinogen, individuals might experience a flashback (a mental experience that mimics an episode of hallucination) as vivid as if they had just taken the drug. Flashbacks can cause panic and hysteria (exaggerated and uncontrollable panic), which can be scary if it happens when users are at work or in another social setting, and dangerous if it happens while they are driving or doing another activity that requires full attention. According to psychiatrist Henry David Abraham, flashbacks are fairly uncommon: "There's a discrete percentage. . . . Maybe one person in 20 will develop serious, continuous problems related to the hallucinogenic experience."[13] However, he adds that for half of those people who experience continual problems, flashbacks can be chronic, lasting years or even their entire lifetime.

J.B., a poster on the MyPTSD message forum website, reveals certain triggers that cause him to flash back to when he first tried LSD. "Whenever I watch certain movies, like *The Doors*, listen to certain music, try to talk about it, or even think about it for very long, I start feeling like I did the day after I did the acid, when I was coming down from it. I get that drained, dried out, hollow head feeling and sometimes I even start shaking. I literally feel like I'm coming down again."[14]

Flashbacks are a periodic but transient experience for some hallucinogen users. Other, more permanent sensory problems brought on by hallucinogen use are part of a condition known as hallucinogen persisting perception disorder (HPPD). "It appears to be a disorder largely of the perceptual system, which is present 24/7," says Abraham, who studies HPPD. "These are folks who can stand on a street corner and a car can drive by, and they'll see a trail of the car. They'll look at a blank wall and see geometric patterns, they'll look at an arm and see a halo around the arm."[15] One patient, Greg W., shared the following experience with HPPD:

In 1974, two weeks after an anxiety-filled LSD trip, I fell into a black hole of panic, crushing depression, terror, horror, and hell. Everything sparkled and glinted with dots like a noisy TV screen. My hand looked like it didn't belong to me. When I moved it, long streaks trailed behind. After looking at the window, when I looked away the lingering afterimage remained for seconds. I was tripping all over again. . . . I came to the terrifying realisation that it was not stopping, and I was going to be all alone on an acid trip for ever.[16]

Greg W.'s life progressed, but the flashbacks did not end, and to this day he still sees things that are not there. He says he has come to realize that "I was indelibly stamped with HPPD and am not who I might have been, but over decades I have overcome it."[17]

Physical Effects on the Body

Hallucinogens have a reputation for interfering with a person's thought processes, but they can also have direct physical effects on the body. Some hallucinogens cause nausea and vomiting before they begin to affect the person's brain. Vomiting is unpleasant but also indicates that the body has recognized whatever substance was just consumed as harmful and is attempting to reject it. Since most hallucinogens are swallowed, they are absorbed into the bloodstream through the digestive tract. However, by the time the body can respond by vomiting, enough of the substance usually has already been absorbed into the bloodstream to begin causing hallucinations or interfering with the person's ability to perceive things properly. The effects of the drug will have already begun and at that point are unstoppable. In the case of most hallucinogens, the effects will carry on for hours or possibly into the next day.

These drugs also interfere with the brain's ability to communicate with the rest of the body through pathways of electrical messages between nerve cells. Because of this, they can cause problems with messages that tell the body's muscles when to tense up and when to relax. Hallucinogens like PCP can cause muscles to clench severely, leading to painful muscle cramps. When muscles cannot relax, a person cannot move and basically loses control of his or her body. The muscles themselves are in danger of becoming overly strained and even permanently damaged in this condition.

"I fell into a black hole of panic, crushing depression, terror, horror, and hell. Everything sparkled and glinted with dots like a noisy TV screen. My hand looked like it didn't belong to me. When I moved it, long streaks trailed behind."[16]

—Greg W., who suffers from HPPD.

Indeed, muscle destruction can be a serious physical side effect of hallucinogen use.

A user's kidneys may also be affected by muscle overactivity brought on by hallucinogen use. The kidneys are organs that filter harmful toxins from the blood. If muscles are overworked through constant contractions, tissue can break down and end up adding toxins to the bloodstream. The resulting toxins may overtax the kidneys and in some cases bring about kidney failure.

The Threat from Overheating

Hallucinogens also raise a person's heart rate, blood pressure, and body temperature. For example, ecstasy is popularly consumed at dance parties because it makes people feel energized and excited, but much of this extra energy comes from the fact that their hearts are beating faster than normal. This can lead to a serious complication called hyperthermia, or overheating of the body (*hyper* means "over" or "in excess," and *thermia* refers to temperature).

> "There is something about seeing a comatose, scantily clad, critically ill teenager who will go on to be brain-dead, which has upset me more than I thought possible."[18]
>
> —Emergency room physician Elizabeth Mitchell.

A person with hyperthermia may sweat heavily and become short of breath. In severe cases hyperthermia leads to heatstroke, a failure of the body's ability to regulate temperature. Heatstroke is a medical emergency that can lead to seizures (surges of electrical activity in the brain), permanent brain damage, and even death. Emergency room physician Elizabeth Mitchell describes treating patients who overdose on ecstasy during raves. "I have worked overnight for several such events and have been truly astounded by what I have seen," she says. "There is something about seeing a comatose, scantily clad, critically ill teenager who will go on to be brain-dead, which has upset me more than I thought possible."[18]

Organizers of parties, concerts, and other events where people tend to use hallucinogens like ecstasy seem to be aware that

Ecstasy is popularly consumed at dance parties and clubs like the one pictured here. The combination of the drug and the hot, crowded conditions can lead to overheating, which can trigger heatstroke that results in seizures, brain damage, and/or death.

overheating is a problem, since they often sell or serve products like ice packs to help people cool down. However, these measures are often inadequate, since life-threating overheating can result from taking just moderate amounts of the drug. Although many users believe they will overheat only if they take large doses, a 2014 study published in the *Journal of Neuroscience* showed that rats fed only moderate doses of ecstasy still experienced dangerous levels of overheating. "Even moderate MDMA doses in conditions that mimic hot, crowded, social settings could be lethal to rats,"[19] reports writer Abby Haglage.

The Myth of Dehydration

Overheating contributed to the death of twenty-year-old Shelley Goldsmith, who collapsed at a concert festival in 2013. Tellingly, however, friends misinterpreted her problem as dehydration. "We thought she was just dehydrated," said Goldsmith's friend Dominique Vletter. "We were all starting to panic until someone said,

Dangers of Drug Combinations

Because a person's body rapidly gets used to hallucinogens, achieving the same level of high can require more of the drug or encourage people to mix hallucinogens with other substances to create a more interesting experience. But mixing substances is a very dangerous practice. Even drugs whose effects are fairly predictable when they are used alone can cause unexpected but drastic reactions when mixed with other drugs or with alcohol.

When mixed together, two drugs can piggyback on each other's effects. If both substances alone would slow down or speed up the body's systems, for example, then combining them might not merely double the effects but increase the body's physical response many times over. Drug combinations can overwhelm the brain, raise blood pressure and heart rate to dangerous levels, prevent the body from controlling its own temperature, or cause serious damage to the liver and kidneys—organs that work to filter substances out of the bloodstream. Since a person in medical distress might not even know what drugs were in the mixture he or she consumed, medical professionals may face great difficulty helping the patient. Mixing drugs, especially hallucinogens that already have unpredictable effects on the body, can seriously endanger a person's health.

'It's OK. It's only dehydration. Nothing could have happened, nothing's wrong. This is all safe.'"[20]

However, Goldsmith was not suffering from dehydration but rather from overheating. And contrary to what most people think, excess water actually *threatens* a person with fatal hyperthermia. "The main mechanism leading to death from psychostimulant drugs appears to be leaking of the brain-blood barrier—which keeps most chemicals in the blood out of the brain—and water accumulation in the brain,'" explains scientist Eugene A. Kiyatkin. Therefore, concertgoers are dangerously mistaken when they think drinking enough water is key to safely taking MDMA. "The excessive use of liquids often used by people at dance clubs could be problematic if they take MDMA," says Kiyatkin. "In addition to its other effects, it inhibits both sweating and urination, which expel water from the body. These factors could also contribute to dangerous water accumulation in the brain."[21] This is what happened to Goldsmith, who died the following evening.

Although drug users tend to abide by the "just stay hydrated and you'll be fine" mythology, health professionals have actually known for decades that hallucinogens like ecstasy can cause the body to retain water in potentially fatal ways. In 1995 fifteen-year-old Anna Wood collapsed at a rave in Australia. Probably aware of the drug's reputation for dehydrating users, she consumed a lot of water throughout her night of dancing. However, she was unaware that ecstasy can slow kidney function, thus keeping her from expelling the water naturally.

She was also unaware that overheating can also interfere with the body's ability to retain a proper balance of salts. Various salts—chemical elements that include sodium and potassium—are always present in the body. Known as electrolytes, they help the body's cells work properly and play important roles in how the nervous system passes electrical messages between the brain and the body. When ecstasy causes the body to retain water, it dilutes these salts and makes them less effective.

The large quantities of water Wood consumed diluted the salts in her blood that are needed to keep water from passing through delicate membranes into areas it does not belong. Water carried by the bloodstream accumulated in her brain and swamped the membranes there, and she died of a cerebral edema (brain swelling) in a nearby hospital. One doctor who reviewed the case said, "Her illness and death bore all the hallmarks of cerebral oedema, and it can be concluded that she died of acute water intoxication, secondary to MDMA ingestion."[22]

Hallucinogens can have many unforeseen and unwanted effects on the body, ranging from unpleasant to dangerous. Hallucinogens' unpredictable nature is what makes them particularly risky. Their reputation as party drugs makes them sound innocent and fun, but it disguises their many underlying dangers.

CHAPTER 3: Hallucinogens and the Potential for Addiction

A major risk of using any drug is that drugs can change how the brain works, often in ways that make the user crave the substance. Such cravings change the lives of people who suffer from them. The brain is tricked into thinking the body needs the drug in order to function normally. As soon as the drug wears off, the person may feel physically ill, shaky, nervous, and sweaty. Headaches, widespread body aches, and digestive problems like vomiting and diarrhea are common. A person can experience psychological issues too, including depression, loneliness, anxiety, or fear. These are typically the opposite of how the person feels while using the drug, which usually deadens feelings of pain and uplifts mood. When the only way the person can avoid feeling miserable is to keep using the drug, he or she has become dependent on it. This is known as a drug addiction.

Addiction can be terribly challenging to overcome. Treating an addiction basically involves retraining the brain and body to function properly again without the presence of the drug. In time the physical pain and sickness the person feels without the drug will lessen and disappear. The psychological issues that can result from addiction, however, are usually much harder to address. It is common for recovering addicts to feel depressed and anxious. They may long for the feelings of happiness and excitement they remember experiencing when using the drug, and this longing might endure for the rest of their life.

Many addicts face an additional social difficulty. Their social support system—the people they turn to and rely on for friendship, companionship, and love—might have vanished during the progression of their drug addiction. Addicts often isolate themselves by lying to or abusing loved ones, abandoning family and friends, losing their jobs, and even doing illegal things like stealing. They become so obsessed with getting more of the drug that little else matters to them. Without anyone telling them to stop, they may not recognize their own dependence.

When trying to recover from a drug addiction, people may find themselves friendless, jobless, and even homeless. This usually worsens their feelings of depression and loneliness, and these individuals might begin using again, thinking it is the only way to feel happy. In this way drug addiction becomes a vicious cycle, one that often ends tragically. Hallucinogens, like any mind-altering substance, can play a leading role in the disastrous development of drug addiction.

People who are trying to recover from drug addiction may experience extreme feelings of depression and loneliness. These feelings can prompt the person to seek relief by resuming drug use, creating a vicious cycle that is difficult to break.

Hallucinogens' Harmless Reputation

When people think of drug addiction, some substances come to mind more than others. Heroin, cocaine, methamphetamine, and alcohol are among the drugs most people associate with addiction, and these substances are so well known in part because of their reputation for causing strong physical dependence. These drugs affect the brain and body in ways that make the user feel very sick when there is not enough of the drug in their bloodstream. The physical symptoms of withdrawal can be severe enough to require medical attention. These substances are widely feared because they are known to cause such a strong (and in many cases fast-forming) physical addiction.

Hallucinogens, on the other hand, are not known to cause physical cravings, at least not to the same degree as drugs like heroin or cocaine. Some hallucinogens—namely PCP—can cause withdrawal symptoms such as headaches and sweating. Ecstasy has also been reported to cause loss of appetite, difficulty sleeping, depression, confusion, rigid muscles, mood swings, and panic attacks when a person stops taking it. In general, however, hallucinogens do not cause physical cravings and withdrawal symptoms the way some drugs do.

Many people assume that because hallucinogens are not physically addicting, they are not dangerous—at least not like heroin, cocaine, or methamphetamine. This is far from true, however. They may not be as physically addicting, but hallucinogens can have very serious mental, emotional, and physical effects on a person's brain and body. Furthermore, their reputation as being somehow less dangerous than other drugs can lead people to take *more* of a hallucinogen in a single dose, believing it is safe. "Because of the physical impact of the drug on the nervous system, their tolerance increases, so they often use more of the drug, use new drugs, or change the way they take the drugs (pills no longer do the trick so they begin using needles),"[23] says addiction researcher David Sheff.

Such behavior is very risky. The effects a hallucinogen could have on the brain and body are always unpredictable. "The direst consequences of drug use aren't reserved exclusively for those who become addicted," says Sheff. "First-time users can wind up in emergency rooms or even dead because they take too much of a drug or take a drug that's been tainted."[24]

The Circle of Dependence

Hallucinogens may not be physically addicting like heroin or cocaine, but they can still have a powerful hold over regular users. For many people they are known to be *psychologically* addicting. Teenagers and young adults, in particular, often begin using hallucinogens while attending concerts, parties, and other social situations. "It is rare for users to take drugs alone," says pharmacologist C.W.M. Wilson. "They are mainly taken with friends or at intimate gatherings."[25] Hallucinogens can make sights and sounds very vivid and interesting and may also lead to feelings of excitement, joy, and friendliness. A person who has used a hallucinogen may feel sociable, likable, funny, attractive, and popular under the effects of the drug.

Such feelings can lead to a psychological dependence on a substance. "When I first started doing drugs, I was around fourteen, going on fifteen," recalled ecstasy user James on the PBS program *In the Mix*. "I'd just moved into a new town, and I wanted to fit in. And that was the way I could fit in that town, by doing drugs. And then it just went from once a month to the weekends, then from the weekends to every day."[26]

> "The direst consequences of drug use aren't reserved exclusively for those who become addicted. First-time users can wind up in emergency rooms or even dead because they take too much of a drug or take a drug that's been tainted."[24]
>
> —Addiction researcher David Sheff.

Memories of feeling like the life of the party make many people want to use a hallucinogen again and again. In fact, they may start to believe they cannot have as much fun at a party or in any social situation unless they take a hallucinogen. The fear of not being funny, good-looking, or likable while sober leads people to think they need the drug. They might also miss the strange way hallucinogens make things look, feel, and sound. "They are in constant search of agents to . . . make life more meaningful, to overcome social inhibitions, and to facilitate meaningful conversations and interpersonal relationships,"[27] Wilson says. When a person reaches this point, going to any social function without first taking the drug can begin to seem daunting. This is a main way hallucinogens reel users into the circle of dependence.

The Dangers of Repeated Use

Not all hallucinogen experiences, or trips, are pleasant. Some can be downright terrifying, and for many people who have used hallucinogens, the overwhelmingly negative experience of a bad trip convinces them not to risk using that drug again. For other people, however, hallucinogen use becomes something of a game. They may use a particular hallucinogen over and over just to see what might happen the next time.

Unfortunately, the human brain quickly adapts to hallucinogens, meaning that the threshold—the amount of the drug necessary to have an effect on senses and perceptions—becomes higher with each use. This means that a person must take greater and greater doses in order to feel the drug's effects. Liam, a journalist from New York, told AlterNet that his first trip on ecstasy at age eighteen involved a warm sensation as well as an inability to feel pain. However, repeated use proved less wonderful. "I continued using and enjoying it, though rarely hit the heights of that intro," he states. "By my early twenties, I was taking several pills once or twice a week at house clubs or parties. But my comedowns became vicious— abject feelings of depression and loneliness at the end of the night."[28] Bad comedowns are only one result of repeated use. The more of the drug that is ingested, the greater the risk it will cause harm to the body or do permanent damage to the brain.

Another potential problem with developing a tolerance to a hallucinogen is that it makes users more likely to experiment with other drugs, often in conjunction with the hallucinogen. "Drugs sold as hallucinogens are frequently mixed with other drugs," says health reporter Diana Hales, "combinations that can produce un-

PCP: The Signs of Addiction

PCP is a commonly used and highly addictive hallucinogen that interferes with brain and central nervous system function. PCP addiction can lead to erratic and aggressive behavior. The symptoms of addiction are often grouped by low–moderate abuse and high-dosage abuse.

Low–moderate PCP abuse can cause:	High-dosage PCP abuse can cause more severe physiological changes such as:	Severe complications of long-term PCP addiction include:
• Increase in breathing rate • Increase in blood pressure • Sweating • Loss of muscle coordination • Delusions • Mild hallucinations • Euphoria • Loss of reality	• Loss of balance • Vomiting • Uncontrolled eye movements • Coma • Seizure • Respiratory distress • Mania	• Difficulty with speech • Memory loss • Depression • Central nervous system damage

Source: Recovery Connection, "PCP Addiction and Withdrawal," 2016. www.recoveryconnection.org.

expected and frightening effects." Marijuana, for example, is often laced (combined) with LSD, PCP, or other hallucinogens before being smoked. "Users often think that the PCP they take together with another illegal psychoactive substance . . . is responsible for the high they feel, so they seek it out specifically,"[29] Hales says. The effects of such drug combinations are even more unpredictable than the effects of taking just one hallucinogen by itself. Furthermore, some substances lead to different physical effects in the body, making it especially dangerous to mix them together. A person who combines one of these drugs with other substances (drugs and alcohol) could create a serious medical emergency.

Could Hallucinogens Be Used to Treat Addiction to Other Drugs?

While some people struggle with addiction to hallucinogens, researchers are wondering whether certain hallucinogens actually have the power to help people addicted to other kinds of drugs. For example, ibogaine, a brown powder derived from a plant called the *Tabernanthe iboga*, has been shown to erase cravings in people addicted to opiates like heroin and morphine. "Rats addicted to morphine will quit for weeks after receiving ibogaine," reports Stanley Glick, director of the Center for Neuropharmacology and Neuroscience at Albany Medical College. Similarly, ayahuasca, a Peruvian plant that naturally contains a hallucinogen known as dimethyltryptamine, has reportedly helped people overcome debilitating addictions to drugs and alcohol.

Both ibogaine and ayahuasca remain illegal and classified as Schedule I drugs because of their unpredictability and potential complications (for example, ibogaine carries an increased risk of cardiac arrest). But substance abuse counselors, scientists, and even addicts themselves are looking into whether these powerful hallucinogens could one day have safe and practical applications.

Quoted in Steven Kotler, "Fighting Drugs with Drugs: An Obscure Hallucinogen Gains Legitimacy as a Solution for Addictions," *Popular Science*, July 21, 2010. www.popsci.com.

The use and dosing of hallucinogens, of course, is rarely if ever scientific. Users make haphazard guesses about how much of a particular substance to ingest and may have no regard for (or even any knowledge of) the possible dangers. Furthermore, many people who produce and sell hallucinogens combine them with cheaper chemicals—some of them poisonous or harmful in their own right—to make more money per dose. Hallucinogens are Schedule I drugs, meaning they are illegal to possess, use, or sell. Therefore, there is no safe and regulated source from which to buy hallucinogens, so users are always at the mercy of the person who produced the drug they are taking. A person who uses hallucinogens might ingest something entirely different than what he or she intended.

Using Hallucinogens to Cope with Other Problems

Not all people who use hallucinogens do so to fit into social situations. Some people who have depression, post-traumatic stress disorder (an anxiety disorder that develops after a terrifying event or ordeal), anxiety, or other problems turn to hallucinogens in an attempt to treat themselves. This is called self-medicating and is a dangerous proposition. Although the first synthetic hallucinogen, LSD, was initially produced and studied as a possible treatment for people with mood disorders such as depression or anxiety, it proved too unpredictable and dangerous to be used as a mainstream treatment. Today when LSD is used experimentally in small doses to treat severe anxiety, its use is closely monitored. When users self-medicate, however, they typically end up becoming dependent on the drug as they try to cope with their other underlying problems.

Dependence develops in the following way: If the drugs seem to help, even temporarily, then individuals are likely to continue to use them in stronger and stronger doses. Hallucinogens provide a temporary escape from people's troubles, and users may begin to believe that they need the drugs to feel normal. Therefore, users are likely to become dependent on the hallucinogens to cope with the stress of life. As spiritual counselor Bridget Clare McKeever says, "Psychological dependence is marked by the inability to cope with ordinary life problems without the drug."[30] Once users begin to seek comfort by removing themselves from reality, they will likely not wish to return to a life full of problems and stress.

> "Psychological dependence is marked by the inability to cope with ordinary life problems without the drug."[30]
>
> —Spiritual counselor Bridget Clare McKeever.

However, drugs merely mask problems; they do not treat them. People who try to treat conditions like post-traumatic stress disorder on their own with hallucinogens may believe they are helping themselves, but in reality they run the risk of becoming dependent on chemicals that can worsen their health and their life. As psychiatrist Elias Dakwar cautions, "Looking to hallucinogens as a way of resolving conflicts or coping with difficulties may not always end on a positive or enlightened note."[31]

Hallucinogens as Gateway Drugs

Because many people believe that hallucinogens are not as dangerous or addictive as other drugs, they may be more willing to experiment with them. If using a hallucinogen turns out to be fun and appears to have no serious effects, a person may be likely to use that same drug again. Not only will the same drug be appealing, but studies show that the person who has tried a particular hallucinogen once or a few times will likely be willing to try another, sometimes harder drug.

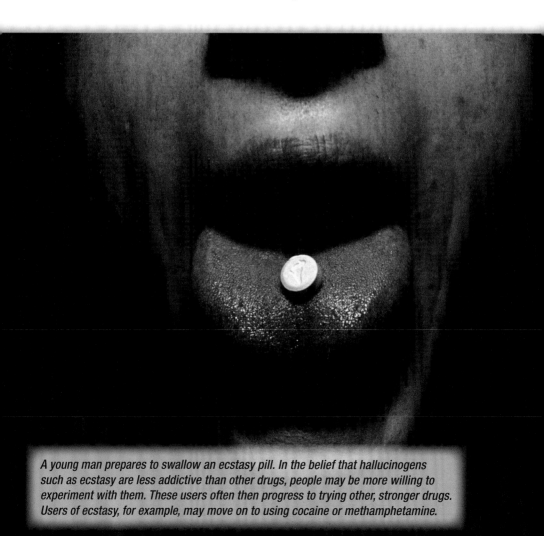

A young man prepares to swallow an ecstasy pill. In the belief that hallucinogens such as ecstasy are less addictive than other drugs, people may be more willing to experiment with them. These users often then progress to trying other, stronger drugs. Users of ecstasy, for example, may move on to using cocaine or methamphetamine.

The Heaviest MDMA User in History

In 2006 doctors from London University began working with a man who is believed to have consumed more ecstasy than any other person in history. Cited in case reports as Mr. A., this British national is estimated to have taken approximately forty thousand MDMA pills over nine years (researchers report that prior to Mr. A, the heaviest known MDMA user on record took two thousand pills over the course of his lifetime).

Mr. A. started using ecstasy at age twenty-one. At first he took an average of five pills per weekend and then was averaging three and a half pills per day. At his peak use, Mr. A. was taking about twenty-five pills per day, which continued for four years. Even after quitting the drug, Mr. A. continues to suffer from severe physical and mental side effects, including severe muscle rigidity in his neck and jaw, which is very painful and makes him unable to open his mouth. He also has paranoia, hallucinations, and depression. Although Mr. A. suffers from extreme short-term memory problems, doctors have been baffled by the fact that his long-term memory remains largely intact. They continue to treat and study Mr. A. in an attempt to learn more about the long-term effects of hallucinogen use.

This phenomenon—starting out with a drug perceived to be fairly safe and progressing step-by-step to stronger drugs—is the reason certain substances are called *gateway drugs*. These are fairly nonaddictive substances that, because of their reputation for having few serious or lasting side effects, tend to be the first drugs the average person will try. Alcohol and marijuana are commonly thought of as gateway drugs.

Hallucinogens do not usually fall into this category, but some research suggests that they may serve in a similar capacity. In a 2006 report, Lesley W. Reid, Kirk W. Elifson, and Claire E. Sterk proposed that ecstasy use may be a precursor to cocaine and methamphetamine use. However, the researchers stipulated that users do not progress from one drug to another because they seek harder drugs, but because they circulate in a scene where all of these drugs are available. Reid, Elifson, and Sterk explain:

> Initiation of ecstasy use . . . may be an initiation into a poly-drug culture in which the availability of other hard drugs is greater and use of such drugs is normalized. In other words, individuals begin to use ecstasy because they perceive it to be low risk, but then put themselves at risk for using other drugs because they have now entered an environment in which polydrug use is common and ecstasy may be adulterated with a variety of other substances unknown to the user.[32]

A Steep Price to Pay

Hallucinogens are often said to be relatively safe and nonaddicting, but this is not always true and can mislead users. "I hear a lot of people talking about Ecstasy, calling it a fun, harmless drug," says a woman named Lynn, who over a five-month period went from living a relatively normal life to being addicted to ecstasy. "All I can think is, 'If they only knew.'" After being unable to sleep, suffering from debilitating headaches, and enduring extreme paranoia, she decided to quit, but only after paying a steep price. "Ecstasy took my strength, my motivation, my dreams, my friends, my apartment, my money and most of all, my sanity. I worry about my future and my health every day."[33] Serious and potentially lifelong complications can accompany the use of these mind-altering substances, and for many people, hallucinogen use can open the door to a world of more frequent and more dangerous drug use.

"Ecstasy took my strength, my motivation, my dreams, my friends, my apartment, my money and most of all, my sanity."[33]

—Lynn, a former ecstasy addict.

CHAPTER 4: Challenges in Treating Hallucinogen Use

Users of hallucinogens often continue their habit because highs are typically temporary and euphoric. Repeated use may reinforce the belief that these drugs are harmless, especially if negative effects (such as headaches or nausea) appear tolerable. It is common for users to remain ignorant—at times willfully so—of hallucinogens' potential dangers until they have a so-called bad trip. But even then, many continue to experiment, hoping to chase pleasurable highs or even hoping that the risk of a future bad trip will be outweighed by the odds of having an enjoyable experience. However, problems resulting from hallucinogen use can persuade some people to seek professional help. They may recognize they are addicted or become aware of the harms of continued use, which prompts them to enroll in a treatment plan to wean themselves from hallucinogens.

Certainly, the choice to leave behind the illusory highs is difficult—as are all decisions to fight addiction—but those who voluntarily seek help are often luckier than those who end up in treatment through mental breakdown or medical emergency—either from a bad trip or a hallucinogenic experience that ends in self-harm. The Drug Abuse Warning Network reports that in 2011 roughly 99 emergency room visits per day involved hallucinogen use among young people aged eighteen to twenty-five. Although this number is low compared to other drug-related emergency room visits (for example, misusers or abusers of prescription and nonprescription pain relievers accounted for 366 visits per day), handling and treating hallucinogen-using patients can prove challenging for even the most experienced medical staff. Before medical workers see such patients, though, they may have to be handled by friends or law enforcement.

Handling Users Who Are Hallucinating

Hallucinogens, especially PCP, can make people aggressive and also resistant to pain. Friends or others who witness someone experiencing a bad trip may not wish to approach or struggle with a user who is enraged or otherwise uncontrollable while under the influence. If the person becomes dangerous to himself or others, bystanders may call the police, and the officers in turn may have no choice but to arrest the person.

If police officers suspect an individual is reacting badly to a drug, they may take him or her to the hospital, where staff might be faced with a violent patient whose physical strength has been enhanced by the drug. Mike Lewter, a former paramedic, describes one male suspect he witnessed being escorted to an emergency room by four police officers. The man was under the influence of PCP and acting aggressively. Lewter says the suspect was thin but still dangerous because he was numbed to pain:

> He had no shirt on which gave a perfect view of the 3 sets of Taser barbs attached to his chest and still connected via thin wires to the Taser units that 3 of the 4 officers were still carrying. That he was hit by 3 separate Taser units was confusing because the guy was about 5'8 and weighed maybe 110–115 [pounds]. Surely this squad of officers who looked like the defensive lineup of the [New Orleans] Saints could handle this little guy. During the process of being checked in, he became rowdy again and all 3 officers triggered their Tasers again which did little more than make the guy giggle.[34]

The patient was put under restraint and given a sedative before he could hurt himself or anyone around him.

Hospital Reponses to Hallucinogen Use

Whenever patients arrive at a hospital after taking some kind of drug, caregivers must immediately assess the situation. In many cases users have overdosed—taken so much of a substance that they become very sick. Some may be unconscious or unresponsive. When users are brought to hospitals in this state, doctors must stabilize them in hopes that they will become responsive. However, many unresponsive patients are dropped off by friends who do not stick around because they fear being questioned by authorities. In these cases, attending physicians have trouble figuring out what exactly the patients have ingested.

Other patients may walk in on their own or be brought in by concerned family or friends. Some of them may be in a state of panic or aggression and perhaps convinced they are in mortal danger. They may think people or monsters are following them or that they are dying. They may believe they can see, hear, or smell things that are not really there, or they may feel terrible pain when

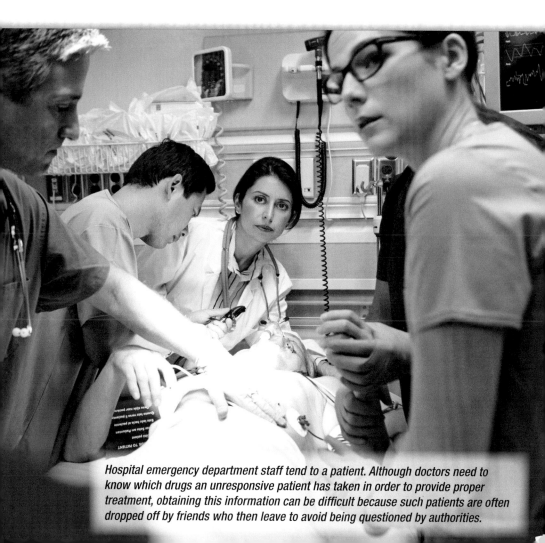

Hospital emergency department staff tend to a patient. Although doctors need to know which drugs an unresponsive patient has taken in order to provide proper treatment, obtaining this information can be difficult because such patients are often dropped off by friends who then leave to avoid being questioned by authorities.

in actuality there is no obvious cause for it. These patients must be calmed so they can help doctors figure out what they took so the right treatment can be administered.

The more challenging patient is the one who resists help. He or she may fight with doctors and staff, fearing that caregivers are trying to do harm. If such an individual panics, he or she may scream, kick, thrash, or try to run away. Physicians Alan J. Gelenberg and Ellen L. Bassuk explain:

Fortunately, most panic reactions are limited to the duration of action of the particular drug used. Since there are no known methods for rapidly eliminating hallucinogenic substances from the body, the primary goal of treatment is to support the patient during this period, mostly by reassuring him that he is not "losing his mind" and that he will soon return to his normal state.[35]

Concerns About Physically Restraining Patients

Physically restraining an aggressive patient can be very challenging and usually requires staff members to work as a team. Patients are typically restrained with straps that prevent them from moving their arms and legs and hurting themselves or others. However, physically restraining a patient who is high on a hallucinogen can itself be dangerous. Restraints can prevent people from breathing normally, for example, and if the drug they have taken is one that already makes them feel short of breath, they are in danger of not getting enough oxygen.

Restraints can also injure people if they struggle against the straps. Their muscles may become strained, and if in a constant state of tension for a long time, they can develop a condition called rhabdomyolysis. In this condition, overly strained muscle tissue rapidly breaks down, the dying muscle cells break open, and their contents spill into the bloodstream. The kidneys, which filter substances out of the blood, can be overwhelmed by the flow of so much unexpected material from the muscle cells. This can lead to kidney damage or even kidney failure, which is a deadly condition. Muscle tissue affected by rhabdomyolysis is also destroyed, which can lead to lifelong complications and disability in those who survive.

Can Hallucinogens Be Used to Treat Fear of Death?

Receiving a terminal diagnosis is one of the most depressing, terrifying, and anxiety-provoking experiences a human can have. Interestingly, researchers are currently looking into whether psilocybin—the active ingredient in hallucinogenic mushrooms—can help such patients face their fear of death and even make their remaining years lighthearted and joyful.

One such person who was treated this way was Patrick Mettes, a fifty-four-year-old who suffered from bile duct cancer. In 2010 Mettes participated in a series of treatment sessions conducted at New York University that involved taking a psilocybin pill under the guidance of a trained therapist. He lay down on a couch and spent the day giving himself over to powerful emotions that included seeing loved ones who had died, appreciating beauty, and feeling reborn. After several sessions, he came to see his cancer as not real, a kind of illusion. He also reported feeling able to live in the present and said he was happier than he had ever been in his whole life.

His wife, Lisa, reported that on his deathbed seventeen months later, he was unafraid, present, and even smiling. As she put it, the psilocybin "allowed him to tap into his own deep resources" to face life's hardest moment with strength and even gratitude. Although such treatments are very experimental and take place under the care of highly trained researchers and scientists, they could offer the terminally ill a different kind of exit.

Quoted in Michael Pollan, "The Trip Treatment," *New Yorker*, February 9, 2015. www.newyorker.com.

Hospital staff must therefore consider the dangers and act ethically in employing such restraints. They must carefully weigh the pros and cons of using restraints, which include protecting themselves from possibly injury and making sure the victim's rights are taken into account. "The use of sedation and restraints is fraught with a host of ethical and legal issues," says pathologist Steven B. Karch. "Safety issues for the patient as well as the medical staff must be considered."[36]

Chemically Restraining Patients

It can be difficult to restrain a patient physically, so medical professionals may turn to chemical restraints to calm a patient who is extremely agitated. Chemical restraints are drugs known to have a calming effect. They are usually given to the patient in pill form or via injection. The drugs most commonly used for agitated patients are benzodiazepines—substances that reduce anxiety, relax muscles, halt seizures, and quell panic attacks. Common benzodiazepines are Valium and Xanax, which are usually very effective at calming a person who is experiencing bad effects from a hallucinogen.

The choice to give benzodiazepines or any other drug to a patient can be risky, however. Medical professionals are often unsure of what other substances the patient has already taken, and benzodiazepines can interact with other chemical substances in unexpected ways. So even though they are known to help patients who have used hallucinogens, these medications may not always be an option if doctors are concerned about drug interactions. Thus, doctors try to obtain all the facts about a case before making a judgment call. When patients are high, however, they may be unable or unwilling to communicate critical information, and doctors must quickly make challenging decisions to stabilize their patients' health.

Difficult Diagnosis

It may be apparent that a patient who arrives at a hospital has taken some type of drug, but what kind is often a mystery. The patient may be too agitated or afraid to answer questions or may

Hallucinogens as a Treatment for Depression and Anxiety

With the exception of marijuana, which has been used to treat certain medical conditions, hallucinogens currently have no accepted medical uses. However, mental health professionals have long been interested in whether hallucinogens might have the potential to help people with conditions like depression or anxiety. Some doctors and scientists think hallucinogenic chemicals, combined with counseling, might be able to help people who are obsessed with negative thoughts find a new way to look at the world. "As counterintuitive as it might seem to treat disorders characterized by obsessive and fixated thinking styles with substances that inspire a loss of control," say psychologists Mitch Earleywine and Mallory Loflin, "anecdotal evidence suggests that obsessive symptoms can be mitigated by hallucinogen treatment."

One difficulty with using hallucinogens to treat medical problems—especially emotional ones—is that the effects of most hallucinogens are unpredictable. Using them could lift someone's spirits but also make the person more anxious or depressed than before. Furthermore, scientists do not fully understand how hallucinogens work in the brain, and they worry these substances could potentially damage chemical receptors. For these reasons, hallucinogens remain classified as illegal substances with no proven or widely used medical benefits, but that could change if certain substances are shown to be effective at treating medical issues without creating additional problems.

Mitch Earleywine and Mallory Loflin, "Therapeutic Hallucinogens: Altered State Laws for Altered States," in *The Psychedelic Policy Quagmire: Health, Law, Freedom, and Society*, ed. J. Harold Ellens and Thomas B. Roberts. Santa Barbara, CA: Praeger, 2015, pp. 328–29.

not even be sure what substance (or combination of substances) he or she took. If other people brought the patient to the hospital, they may not know what the person took or may not be honest about it. Hallucinogens are illegal, and if friends bring a patient to the hospital for help, they might lie to avoid getting their friend or themselves in trouble.

Not knowing what drug patients took, how much of it they took, or how long ago they took it makes it difficult for hospital workers to diagnose and treat the problem. Since some medications interact in harmful ways, not knowing what else a patient has taken can limit options for treatment. In some cases hospital workers can take a blood or urine sample and perform a toxicity screen—a chemical test that identifies certain substances in a person's body fluids. However, only some hallucinogens reliably show up on toxicity screens. LSD and mushrooms, for example, are not always detected, and even if some signs appear, it may be difficult for doctors to clearly identify a substance.

In one case a twenty-year-old woman was brought into a Syracuse, New York, emergency room unconscious and unresponsive. The doctor on call ordered a urine test that revealed the presence of amphetamines in the body, but those would not account for her unresponsiveness. She also had dangerously low sodium levels, which if untreated could lead to serious brain damage or death. Only by searching the patient's cell phone records did family members discover the young woman had used ecstasy. Without that piece of information, the doctor was unable to diagnose the woman's condition. The doctor ordered the administration of a sodium solution and the woman recovered, but such problems suggest how difficult it can be for caregivers to provide proper and timely treatment for some patients.

Even if the patient has used a substance that a toxicity screen can identify, it might still be difficult or impossible to collect blood or urine from a patient who is agitated, panicked, or upset after using a hallucinogen. Since doctors rely on these tests to identify which substance—or mixture of substances—are in the patient's body, not obtaining a sample in a timely manner can impact the patient's health. Administering the wrong antidote or prescribing an ineffective treatment because an unsettled patient refuses to cooperate will worsen his or her condition.

Long-Term Treatment

In many cases, hospital workers observe patients until the drug's effects wear off and the patient can safely go home. In serious cases, such as when the patient has had a severe physical reaction to a drug, a longer hospital stay might be needed. A patient may be sent to a psychiatric hospital—one that specifically treats mental disorders—until the drug's effects wear off and a doctor determines it is safe for the patient to leave.

Treatment at a recovery facility may also be needed. Some patients may be remanded (ordered by a court or otherwise forced to go) to such facilities; others may seek help there on their own. Because hallucinogen users often come to depend on drugs to help them cope with underlying emotional issues, they can benefit from counseling, which recovery facilities typically provide. Therapists help patients identify the underlying problems that made them turn to hallucinogens. These include depression, anxiety, feeling uncertain in social situations, or any of the varied reasons a person might begin using hallucinogens.

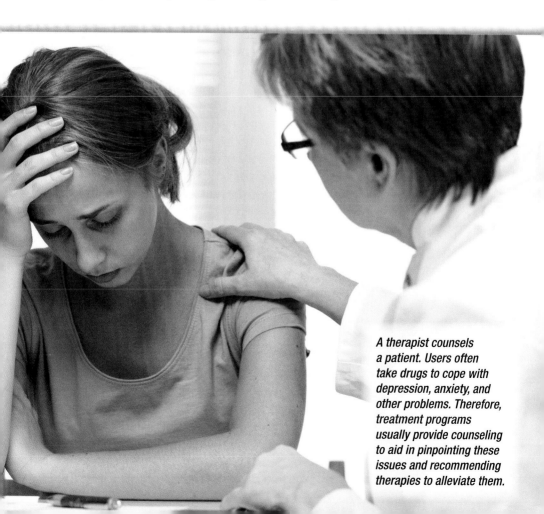

A therapist counsels a patient. Users often take drugs to cope with depression, anxiety, and other problems. Therefore, treatment programs usually provide counseling to aid in pinpointing these issues and recommending therapies to alleviate them.

The Morningside Recovery facility in Orange County, California, institutes a treatment process that involves psychiatric and psychological assessments of patients to figure out what kind of treatment plan is needed. The clinicians then chart a plan tailored to each individual that includes working alone with a therapist and spending time in group sessions to talk about his or her experiences. The therapists employ cognitive behavioral therapy (CBT) to help patients discover the source of their problems and the strategies they employed to avoid dealing with them. Once these are identified, patients can learn new methods of coping in order to resist the temptation to escape into a hallucinatory world. According to the Morningside Recovery website, "Clients receiving treatments for hallucinogens find that CBT provides not only the personal insight they were perhaps seeking with drugs but offers 'thinking tools' to use in everyday life. These tools help them meet the world on realistic terms, instead of seeking a temporary alternate reality."[37] Other facilities may use similar methods or create varied treatment plans to address their clients' needs.

> "CBT provides [patients] not only the personal insight they were perhaps seeking with drugs but offers 'thinking tools' to use in everyday life. These tools help them meet the world on realistic terms, instead of seeking a temporary alternate reality."[37]
>
> —Morningside Recovery, a rehabilitation facility.

Treatments for hallucinogen dependence work best if they are sustained over a long time and do not include the expectation that users will remain abstinent throughout the recovery period. Importantly, studies show that treatment plans work. According to *Psychology Today*, "Patients who stay in treatment longer than three months usually have better outcomes than those who stay for a shorter time. Patients who go through medically assisted withdrawal to minimize discomfort but do not receive any further treatment perform about the same in terms of their drug use as those who were never treated."[38] Users who stay involved with treatment learn strategies to resist reabusing, and typically they are able to move forward with their lives.

The Effort to Stay Clean

The 2011 Treatment Episode Data Set, a national demographic resource of the Center for Behavioral Health Statistics and Quality, reports that in that year (the last for which data were available), 403,756 persons aged eighteen to twenty-five were admitted to treatment facilities. No data is available specific to hallucinogen users who were admitted, but the number is likely somewhere under thirty-two individuals per day (which is the number of persons admitted for use of "other drugs" not categorized as opiates, marijuana, alcohol, stimulants, or cocaine).

There are no statistics for the number of hallucinogen users who return to drugs after either leaving treatment early or successfully completing such programs. However, reuse, or recidivism, is a real concern, since many users return to lives that are still filled with pressing problems, peer pressure, and easy access to drugs. Even though they may have learned about the dangers of drug use—or experienced them firsthand—the lure of hallucinogen highs can be strong. As a sixteen-year-old former ecstasy user named Angie told PBS's *In the Mix*, "It's unbelievably hard for me not to pick up any drugs, but I take it one day at a time, pray to and thank my higher-power, and I always remember where I came to this point from, which I could not imagine going back to."[39]

Some users, however, may again seek escape in hallucinogens, or they might redirect their urge to use by abusing other substances. "Increased alcohol use is often reported by patients to reduce their symptoms,"[40] say psychiatrists Michael B. First and Allan Tasman. Masking the urge to reabuse hallucinogens with other substances may end up worsening the problems that originally led users to abuse. Continuing with treatment usually reinforces what users need to know to stay clear of drugs and teaches them coping strategies to avoid turning to alcohol or other substances to manage life's problems. Some might have to make several visits to rehabilitation clinics in order to move forward with their lives.

Users who are honest with themselves about the temptation to reabuse drugs discover that coping with dependence on substances often requires significant time and effort. For most people, this is a lifelong struggle, since the desire to take drugs can resurface anytime something depressing or difficult happens. Long-term treatment for hallucinogen use is usually far more challenging than treating the immediate consequences of an episode of drug use that has gone badly. Staying clean requires the will to face real-world problems drug free. It also requires the self-awareness to acknowledge that the temptation to return to the euphoria of the world of hallucinogens will persist through sobriety.

CHAPTER 5: Preventing the Abuse of Hallucinogens

Drug abuse prevention has been a topic of political and social concern for years. As hallucinogens and other drugs hit the streets, stories of bad trips and overdoses surface, leaving medical, law enforcement, and civic leaders to strategize ways to combat the new trend. Most authorities agree that prevention is better than incarceration, so government and local efforts focus on programs that seek to educate people about the dangers of drugs. The US government has helped create many such programs, which are often launched in schools and elsewhere in communities to spread the message that hallucinogen use is risky and potentially life-threatening.

Making Hallucinogens Illegal

After the US government briefly experimented with social and medical applications for hallucinogens in the 1950s and 1960s, various states, beginning with California in 1966, outlawed hallucinogen possession, sale, and use. Other states followed suit throughout the 1960s, first banning LSD, then mushrooms and peyote. Finally, the federal passage of the Controlled Substances Act in 1970 specifically prohibited the manufacture, possession, and distribution of a host of drugs, including hallucinogens. Of all the hallucinogens, only peyote is given a special exemption from legal prosecution if it is used as part of Native American religious rituals.

As with most illicit drugs, however, banning hallucinogens has not prevented their continued sale and use. In the United States, although the threat of incarceration may be a deterrent, the federal government—along with state leaders, local authorities, civic organizations, schools, and religious groups—has sought other ways to dissuade people from using drugs. The National Institute on Drug Abuse (NIDA), a federal research organization within the US Department of Health and Human Services, helps coordinate drug-prevention efforts at the local level, where such programs can reach vulnerable groups—such as teenagers—within communities. NIDA offers guidelines to assist local authorities in devising prevention strategies, but typically these efforts are aimed at drug use in general and are not often targeted at hallucinogens specifically.

The Substance Abuse and Mental Health Services Administration (SAMHSA), another arm of the US Department of Health and Human Services, provides some basics on the dangers of hallucinogen use and encourages teens to know the law and the facts about the drugs. A critical point SAMHSA makes is that despite the fact that some young people think everyone tries these drugs at some point, the vast majority have actually stayed away from them. In fact, SAMHSA cites research that found that "96 percent of 12- to 17-year-olds have never even tried hallucinogens."[41] SAMHSA advises teens to learn the signs of hallucinogen use so they can tell whether their friends have been using and, if so, to get them the help they need.

> "[Ninety-six] percent of 12- to 17-year-olds have never even tried hallucinogens."[41]
>
> —SAMHSA

The Importance of Teaching Prevention in Schools and at Home

Much of NIDA's and SAMHSA's efforts focus on school-age children, and to this end NIDA trains local leaders (or teachers) to speak at schools and conduct workshops for classes or groups of educators. Lectures or workshops for students emphasize risk factors for drug use; those for educators describe how to assess whether students might be using hallucinogens or other drugs. Convincing young people never to try a hallucinogen or other substance at all is far easier than helping those who have already become hooked on them. "The age group that is most likely to experiment with illicit drugs are teenagers and young adults," says psychology profes-

Because teenagers and young adults are more likely than members of other age groups to experiment with illicit drugs, the strongest prevention efforts are aimed at teens like the ones shown here. These often include school presentations that provide factual information intended to discourage young people from trying drugs in the first place.

sor Thomas C. Rowe. "The real place to reach them is through the schools. The earlier the effort starts, the better."[42]

This is why the strongest drug-prevention efforts are typically put forth in schools. Behavioral researchers tend to agree that the best way to stem hallucinogen use is to provide clear, accurate, science- or research-based information about drugs. "If you provide any age group with understandable and accurate information it is likely that the majority . . . will choose not to experiment with that drug,"[43] says Rowe.

Southeastern Louisiana University kinesiology and health studies professors Ralph Wood and Linda B. Synovitz assert that bolstering students' life skills—which include confidence, self-esteem, and decision-making and problem-solving skills—is key in helping young people resist drugs. In their opinion, prevention efforts should not only discuss the dangers of hallucinogens but also reinforce students' social skills and self-esteem so that they will be able to handle or be immune to the pressures that lead many to try the drugs.

Wood and Synovitz also think that educators and school staff should not just be teaching students—they should be observing them for signs of drug use. These include physical education teachers who could "monitor student conversations in the locker room" and "student behavior during physical activity exercises," nurses who can spot specific effects of ecstasy or other drugs, and counselors who should "monitor changes in student grades, behavior, and mood."[44] Wood and Synovitz suggest that these authorities should work together with families and the larger community.

Enlisting Families' Help

Having a family that knows about drug abuse and is attentive to children's physical and mental needs is an important part of drug prevention. Studies show that children and teenagers who have a strong system of support at home—including a network of parents, relatives, and family friends whom they feel they can trust and depend on—are far less likely to try drugs than young people who do not feel they have a dependable network. Parents and other guardians are most effective in preventing drug use when they are aware of their children's attitudes toward others, their performance in school, and their willingness to behave unwisely.

To this end, parents are advised to become aware of factors that may predispose their children to experiment with hallucinogens. "Predisposing risk factors are both personal and situational," say educational psychologists Harry Ayers and Cesia Prytys. "Personal factors include preexisting emotional and (behavioral) problems, learning disabilities, school failure, risk taking activities and positive attitudes toward drug taking." They note that parenting styles can also affect a teenager's likelihood of trying drugs. "Some parents fail to lay down and enforce rules about drug use and do not adequately supervise their children,"[45] Ayers and Prytys say, leaving children too much room to experiment.

The NIDA-endorsed Strengthening Families Program is one option for parents who need help reaching their children. The program invites parents and children ages ten to fourteen to community meeting places where—over seven two-hour sessions—counselors guide them in learning communication skills, ways to resist peer pressure, and the harms of substance abuse. Although NIDA and other drug authorities have programs that parents can investigate to help deter children from taking or abusing hallucinogens or other illicit substances, firm parental supervision remains the most common and dependable frontline method of prevention.

Program Success and Criticism

Even if not all people are dissuaded from experimenting with hallucinogens, NIDA attests that science-based drug-prevention programs work. "When research-based substance use prevention

Exclusions for Religion

Peyote is the only hallucinogen for which there is a legal exemption. In 1991 two men in Oregon were denied unemployment benefits because drug tests showed they had used the hallucinogen mescaline (the drug derived from the peyote cactus). The men belonged to the Native American Church, which uses peyote in religious ceremonies and rituals. The case went to the Supreme Court, which ultimately ruled that religious traditions involving peyote were not protected by the US Constitution.

In 1994, however, President Bill Clinton signed a law that stated federal and state regulation of controlled substances did not apply to peyote when used for religious purposes. Thus, centuries-old religious traditions involving the psychedelic cactus were deemed legally permissible in the United States. Use of peyote by other groups or for recreational purposes, however, remains illegal.

programs are properly implemented by schools and communities, use of alcohol, tobacco, and illegal drugs is reduced,"[46] the organization maintains. Not all reviewers of drug-prevention programs are so supportive, however. Some note that the programs used in schools and communities vary widely and often suffer from different degrees of funding. Poor rural areas, for example, may not have the resources to institute programs that require paid counselors or speakers. In some cases drug-prevention programs may have been implemented in an area but not updated to deal with emerging drug scenes.

Although NIDA promotes evidence-based prevention programs (in which students are routinely surveyed to discover drug trends), not all school drug-prevention programs follow that model. Lisa L. Sample, a professor of public affairs and community service at the University of Nebraska–Omaha, and Crystal Fuller, a manager of substance-abuse-prevention services for five Nebraska counties, note that the Drug Abuse Resistance Education (D.A.R.E.) programs begun in the 1980s are still in use in many counties across the United States. But they point out that these programs have not kept pace with drug trends or the specific drug abuse problems of different geographic locations. Sample and Fuller state, "The types of drugs children are pressured to use have changed considerably since the 1980s and 1990s, when many drug-prevention programs like DARE were developed. The use of crack cocaine has declined overall, for example, while the misuse of prescription drugs materialized in the last 10 years and continues to increase."[47] The demographics of drug use among teens have changed as well, and it is critical that drug-prevention programs have up-to-date information on who is using what kind of drug. Sample and Fuller maintain that, as school budgets are slashed, it is important for remaining resources to be channeled into programs that reflect contemporary changes in drug usage.

Harm Reduction

In lieu of preventing hallucinogen use, some organizations have tried an approach known as harm reduction. Harm-reduction programs and policies do not try to prevent, or even reduce, use;

A police officer raises a banner advertising a carnival to promote D.A.R.E., which stands for Drug Abuse Resistance and Education. D.A.R.E. was developed in the 1980s and is still used in many parts of the United States to combat drug use. Critics, however, complain that the program has not kept up with current drug trends.

rather, they aim to help people use drugs or engage in other high-risk activities in as safe a way as possible. The philosophy underlying harm-reduction programs is that people are going to use drugs no matter what—the goal is to get them to do so in a way that poses the least amount of harm to themselves or others. Examples of harm-reduction programs include needle exchanges (in which intravenous drug users turn in used, dirty needles for clean ones, in the hopes of curbing the spread of disease); condom distribution programs in high schools (which opponents argue promotes underage sex but supporters say promotes safe sex); and, in the case of hallucinogens, groups or programs that provide materials, products, or information that is intended to reduce the likelihood of a medical emergency.

One hallucinogen-related harm-reduction group is DanceSafe, which was founded in 1998. The group approaches hallucinogen use as inevitable—and if people are going to use these drugs,

DanceSafe believes they should do so in as safe an environment as possible. "It's unrealistic to think we can keep drugs out of clubs and bars and festivals. Trying to do that causes more harm than good," says DanceSafe executive director Missi Wooldridge. "We need to be realistic and recognize drug use first and foremost as a health concern."[48] The group feels it is more important to provide information about what a drug does, how it works, and how a person can avoid having a negative experience. "It's important to talk about that and prevent medical emergencies,"[49] says Wooldridge.

> "It's unrealistic to think we can keep drugs out of clubs and bars and festivals. Trying to do that causes more harm than good."[48]
>
> —DanceSafe executive director Missi Wooldridge.

To this end, members of DanceSafe go to music festivals, where they pass out information about MDMA and other hallucinogens typically present in those environments. They also pass out water and electrolyte-infusion cocktails, and they even sell drug-testing kits. The kits, which cost sixty-five dollars, allow potential users to test the substance they are about to take to see if it is cut with other harmful ingredients. At other events, DanceSafe has reportedly set up booths where people can bring pills to be tested. "Mostly when people come to us with a sample, it's because they bought Molly and they want to know if it is MDMA or something else that could be potentially more harmful," says Wooldridge of how people use the booths. "The biggest issue when we see medical emergencies is that it's been highly cut, highly adulterated with something else."[50]

Because harm-reduction strategies do not condemn drug use, and in many instances even facilitate it, it is a very controversial strategy. Opponents of DanceSafe and other hallucinogen-related harm-reduction organizations claim that by supporting drug use, it sends the message that there are safe and risk-free ways to do these drugs—which is impossible to say of substances as unpredictable as hallucinogens. For this reason, harm-reduction strategies have not been adopted en masse, and laws exist that hinder their ability to function at events.

Legislative Efforts

Indeed, the presence of groups like DanceSafe at raves and clubs is complicated by a piece of legislation known as the Illicit Drug Anti-Proliferation Act, better known as the Reducing Americans' Vulnerability to Ecstasy (RAVE) Act. The act was passed in 2003 and sponsored in part by then senator Joe Biden. The RAVE Act makes club owners and concert promoters criminally liable if they

Should It Be a Felony to Use Hallucinogens as Date-Rape Drugs?

Hallucinogens such as ketamine have been used as date-rape drugs, which are substances given to other people (usually women) without their knowledge. Often, a date-rape drug is added to a woman's beverage. Once it dissolves, it has no odor or taste and usually goes undetected by the victim. After she ingests it, she may hallucinate or become unaware of her surroundings. She may feel sluggish and find it hard to move. Her social inhibitions disappear, and she may agree to have sex with whoever drugged her or be unaware she is doing so.

Preventing this criminal use of hallucinogens remains a priority for law enforcement officials, but their ability to press felony charges against someone who uses a date-rape drug has been challenged by changes to laws in places like California. For example, Proposition 47, passed in 2014, inadvertently removed felony charges for date-rape drugs by grouping them in with recreational drug offenses. It did so as an attempt to decriminalize certain kinds of drug use, which can help communities free up space in jails and spend money on drug treatment programs, which are often underfunded. But in the case of Proposition 47, it ended up creating a loophole in which using a date-rape drug on someone became a misdemeanor. "Date-rape drugs are used for one reason—to commit sexual assault," said California State Assembly member Marc Steinorth. The task before California and other states is to find ways to decriminalize certain kinds of drug use but retain appropriate punishments for others.

Quoted in Jeff Horseman, "Prop. 47: Bill Would Turn Date-Rape Drugs Back into Felony," *Riverside (CA) Press Enterprise*, February 24, 2015. www.pe.com.

are found to be encouraging drug use. The law was intended to motivate club owners to crack down on drug sales that might take place on their property or during their event, but its effect has been to curb the extent to which organizations like DanceSafe can practice harm-reduction strategies at music festivals, concerts, and other spaces where drugs are often taken.

Believing that limiting the work of harm-reduction groups drives drug use further underground—and thus makes it more dangerous—Dede Goldsmith is one person fighting to change the RAVE Act. After her daughter, Shelley, died from ecstasy in 2013, Goldsmith became committed to the idea that had her daughter had more information about drug safety and access to resources such as on-site drug testing, her life might have been saved. To this end, in 2014, on the one-year anniversary of Shelley's death, Goldsmith launched the Amend the RAVE Act campaign. She writes on her organization's website:

> The goal of the campaign is . . . to make [electronic dance music] festivals and concerts safer for our young people. . . . I am asking for language to be added to the law to make it clear that event organizers and venue owners can implement safety measures to reduce the risk of medical emergencies, including those associated with drug use, without fear of prosecution by federal authorities.[51]

Those changes have not yet been adopted, but other parents have attempted similar legislative actions to address problems they think contributed to their child's destructive experience with a drug. One parent (whose identity has been kept from the public) had the horrific experience of being called to the Upstate University Hospital in Syracuse, New York, in 2012 because her twenty-year-old daughter had been brought unresponsive to the emergency room. The girl had been dropped off that morning by a man who said only that they had gone to a concert together—he then left the hospital.

The girl was comatose, incontinent, vomiting, and brain damaged. She woke up a week later and had to learn to read, write,

Singer Jon Bon Jovi, whose daughter survived a heroin overdose, attends an event marking the passage of a Good Samaritan law in New Jersey. These types of laws protect anyone who assists medical personnel in aiding an overdose victim from prosecution for criminal wrongdoing.

and talk all over again. From looking through her phone messages it became clear that she had taken ecstasy—but because the man who dropped her at the hospital offered no information about what she took, how much, or when, doctors had to run test after test to figure out what the problem was, wasting valuable time. Dr. Lisa Sanders explains that the man's lack of information critically compromised the girl's life. "The young woman had been dangerously ill for some time—possibly hours before anyone took her to the E.R. Why? Were her friends afraid that they might be arrested if they revealed that they used drugs the night before? Had they not worried about getting in trouble, perhaps they would have taken her earlier."[52]

Therefore, with the help of her state legislators and other activists, the girl's mother lobbied for New York to adopt a Good Samaritan law. This kind of law, which exists in Washington, Connecticut, and New Mexico, protects those who seek medical help for someone who has overdosed. It prevents so-called Good Samaritans from being prosecuted for criminal wrongdoing if they cooperate with medical personnel to get the person the help they need. The law successfully passed in 2013, and according to Dr. Sharon Stancliff, medical director for the Harm Reduction Coalition, it "sends a very strong message to law enforcement and the general public that saving lives is much more important than putting people into the criminal justice system."[53]

Setting Realistic Goals

It is unrealistic to expect that passing and enforcing laws against drugs like hallucinogens will make them vanish from society. At best, such policies can be combined with drug education and prevention programs to discourage would-be users from experimenting with such substances. It is not always possible to prevent people from trying or using drugs, but lessening the number or amount of substances they do use and minimizing the effects on their life and health is a worthwhile aim.

If education programs can encourage people who do use hallucinogens to moderate their activity, the risks of using hallucinogens might be reduced. In addition, these programs might convince others not to pick up the drugs at all. Harm reduction strategies are devised not to eliminate drug use but to educate as many people as possible about the potential dangers associated with hallucinogens and other drugs so that people can make better, more reasoned choices once they know the risks.

SOURCE NOTES

Chapter 1: Hallucinogens: The Scope of the Problem

1. Quoted in Paul May, "Lysergic Acid Diethylamide—LSD," University of Bristol School of Chemistry, December 1998. www.chm.bris.ac.uk.
2. Steven B. Karch and Olaf Drummer, *Karch's Pathology of Drug Abuse*, 5th ed. Boca Raton, FL: CRC, 2016, p. 700.
3. Passingtime, "Bad Acid Trip!," Experience Project, May 20, 2009. www.experienceproject.com.
4. Drug Enforcement Administration, "Drug Schedules." www.dea.gov.

Chapter 2: Effects of Using Hallucinogens

5. Frank F. Daly and Luke Yip, "Phencyclidine and Hallucinogen Poisoning," in *Irwin and Rippe's Intensive Care Medicine*, 6th ed., ed. Richard S. Irwin and James M. Rippe. Philadelphia: Wolters Kluwer, 2008, p. 1682.
6. Daly and Yip, "Phencyclidine and Hallucinogen Poisoning," pp. 1681–82.
7. Quoted in Justin Peters, "This Month in PCP: Naked Guys, Car Chases, and Big Jugs of Sweet Tea (That Are Full of PCP)," *Slate*, March 29, 2013. www.slate.com.
8. DXMMan, "Very Very Weird!," Erowid, April 12, 2008. www.erowid.org.
9. Terry Rustin, "Substance Abuse," in *Emergency Psychiatry: Principles and Practice*, ed. Rachel L. Glick et al. Philadelphia: Wolters Kluwer, 2008, p. 248.
10. Quoted in *In the Mix*, "Ashley's Story," PBS. www.pbs.org.
11. Quoted in Jessica Savage, "Police: Hotel Jumper on PCP," *Lufkin (TX) News*, December 8, 2008. www.lufkindailynews.com.

12. Chuck Joyner, *Advanced Concepts in Defensive Tactics: A Survival Guide for Law Enforcement*. Boca Raton, FL: CRC, 2011, p. 211.
13. Quoted in Shaunacy Ferro, "Are Acid Flashbacks a Myth?," *Popular Science*, September 23, 2013. www.popsci.com.
14. J.B., "Acid Flashbacks?," MyPTSD, July 1, 2011. www.myptsd .com.
15. Henry David Abraham, "When the Trip Doesn't End," *Psychologist*, September 2014, p. 672.
16. Quoted in Abraham, "When the Trip Doesn't End," p. 672.
17. Quoted in Abraham, "When the Trip Doesn't End," p. 672.
18. Quoted in Rong-Gong Lin II and Sarah Ardalani, "Death at Electric Daisy Carnival Draws Attention to Connection Between Raves and Ecstasy," *Los Angeles Times*, July 5, 2010. http://articles.latimes .com.
19. Abby Haglage, "Why Molly Is Especially Deadly at Summer Music Festivals," *Daily Beast*, June 7, 2014. www.thedailybeast.com.
20. Quoted in Haglage, "Why Molly Is Especially Deadly at Summer Music Festivals."
21. Quoted in Haglage, "Why Molly Is Especially Deadly at Summer Music Festivals."
22. Brad Clifton, "Hug Ends Anguish for Woods," *Daily Telegraph* (Sydney, Australia), June 19, 1996. www.dailytelegraph.com.au.

Chapter 3: Hallucinogens and the Potential for Addiction

23. David Sheff, *Clean: Overcoming Addiction and Ending America's Greatest Tragedy*. Boston: Houghton Mifflin Harcourt, 2013, p. 79.
24. Sheff, *Clean*, p. 77.
25. C.W.M. Wilson, *The Pharmacological and Epidemiological Aspects of Adolescent Drug Dependence*. Oxford: Pergamon, 2013, p. 447.
26. Quoted in *In the Mix*, "James' Story," PBS. www.pbs.org.
27. Wilson, *The Pharmacological and Epidemiological Aspects of Adolescent Drug Dependence*, p. 447.
28. Quoted in Tony O'Neill, "My First Time on Ecstasy: 10 True Tales," AlterNet, May 2, 2014. www.alternet.org.
29. Diana Hales, *An Invitation to Health*, 12th ed. Belmont, CA: Thomson Wadsworth, 2007, p. 329.

30. Bridget Clare McKeever, *Hidden Addictions: A Pastoral Response to the Abuse of Legal Drugs*. New York: Routledge, 2013, eBook.

31. Elias Dakwar, "Hallucinogens: The Mind Field of Oswald," in *The Addiction Casebook*, ed. Petros Levounis and Abigail J. Herron. Washington, DC: American Psychiatric, 2014, p. 80.

32. Lesley W. Reid, Kirk W. Elifson, and Claire E. Sterk, "Ecstasy and Gateway Drugs: Initiating the Use of Ecstasy and Other Drugs," *Annals of Epidemiology*, January 2007, p. 6.

33. Quoted in Drug-Free World, "Is Ecstasy Addictive? Get the Facts on MDMA Addiction." www.drugfreeworld.org.

Chapter 4: Challenges in Treating Hallucinogen Use

34. Mike Lewter, "What Are Some of the Craziest Emergency Room (ER) Stories, as Told by the Nurses and Doctors Who Work There?," *Quora* (blog). www.quora.com.

35. Alan J. Gelenberg and Ellen L. Bassuk, eds., *The Practitioner's Guide to Psychoactive Drugs*, 4th ed. New York: Springer Science + Business Media, 2013, p. 338.

36. Steven B. Karch, ed., *Addiction and the Medical Complications of Drug Abuse*. Boca Raton, FL: CRC, 2008, p. 88.

37. Morningside Recovery, "Hallucinogen Addiction Treatment," 2014. www.morningsiderecovery.com.

38. *Psychology Today*, "Hallucinogens," November 24, 2014. www.psychologytoday.com.

39. Quoted in *In the Mix*, "POV: Ecstasy and Club Drugs," PBS. www.pbs.org.

40. Michael B. First and Allan Tasman, *Clinical Guide to the Diagnosis and Treatment of Mental Disorders*, 2nd ed. Hoboken, NJ: Wiley, 2010, p. 199.

Chapter 5: Preventing the Abuse of Hallucinogens

41. Substance Abuse and Mental Health Services Administration, "Tips for Teens: Hallucinogens," 2008. www.samhsa.gov.

42. Thomas C. Rowe, *Federal Narcotics Laws and the War on Drugs: Money down a Rat Hole*. Binghamton, NY: Haworth, 2006, p. 158.

43. Rowe, *Federal Narcotics Laws and the War on Drugs*, p. 158.

44. Ralph Wood and Linda B. Synovitz, "Addressing the Threats of MDMA (Ecstasy): Implications for School Health Professionals, Parents, and Community Members," *Journal of School Health*, January 2001, p. 41.

45. Harry Ayers and Cesia Prytys, *An A to Z Practical Guide to Emotional and Behavioural Difficulties*. New York: Routledge, 2012, p. 5.

46. National Institute on Drug Abuse, "Preventing Drug Abuse: The Best Strategy," 2009. www.drugabuse.gov.

47. Lisa L. Sample and Crystal Fuller, "Why Static, One-Size-Fits-All School Drug-Prevention Programs Don't Work," *Governing*, June 3, 2013. www.governing.com.

48. Quoted in Phillip Smith, "If You're Going to Take Ecstasy for New Year's Play It Safe," AlterNet, December 17, 2014. www1.alternet.org.

49. Quoted in Katy Moeller, "With Feel-Good Drug Molly, the Party Can Turn Deadly," *Idaho Statesman* (Boise, ID), April 10, 2015. www.idahostatesman.com.

50. Quoted in Moeller, "With Feel-Good Drug Molly, the Party Can Turn Deadly."

51. Dede Goldsmith "About the Campaign," Amend the RAVE Act. www.amendtheraveact.org.

52. Lisa Sanders, "In the Case of an Unresponsive Woman, Text Messages Offer Clues," *New York Times*, October 12, 2012. www.nytimes.com.

53. Quoted in Maia Szalavitz, "New York State Passes 'Good Samaritan' Law to Fight Overdose," *Time*, July 29, 2011. http://healthland.time.com.

American Society of Addiction Medicine (ASAM)

4601 N. Park Ave.
Upper Arcade, Suite 101
Chevy Chase, MD 20815
phone: (301) 656-3920 • fax: (301) 656-3815
website: www.asam.org

ASAM exists to educate physicians, other health care providers, and the public about drug addictions and to support research on and prevention of drug abuse.

Community Anti-Drug Coalitions of America (CADCA)

625 Slaters Ln., Suite 300
Alexandria, VA 22314
phone: (800) 522-2322
website: www.cadca.org

CADCA is a nonprofit organization that works with communities in the United States and eighteen other countries to prevent alcohol, tobacco, and other drug abuse on a local level.

DanceSafe

800 Grant St., Suite 110
Denver, CO 80203
phone: (888) 636-2411
website: www.dancesafe.org

DanceSafe is a public health organization that informs young people about ways to stay safe in the electronic dance community. It is peer based and focused on harm reduction through education. Its website has information on the hazards of club drugs and minimizing risks associated with their use.

Drug Free America Foundation, Inc.
5999 Central Ave., Suite 301
Saint Petersburg, FL 33710
phone: (727) 828-0211 • fax: (727) 828-0212
website: http://dfaf.org

This drug-prevention and drug-policy organization develops and promotes policies to reduce illegal drug use and drug addiction.

Drug Watch International
PO Box 45218
Omaha, NE 68145
phone: (402) 384-9212
website: www.drugwatch.org

Drug Watch International aids drug-prevention efforts worldwide by providing science-based information on harmful substances and by opposing efforts to legalize drugs.

National Center on Addiction and Substance Abuse (CASA)
633 Third Ave., 19th Floor
New York, NY 10017
phone: (212) 841-5200
website: www.centeronaddiction.org

CASA is a national nonprofit organization that conducts research to inform the public about, improve health care for, and recommend policies on substance use and addiction.

National Council on Alcoholism and Drug Dependence (NCADD)
217 Broadway, Suite 712
New York, NY 10007
phone: (212) 269-7797 • fax: (212) 269-7510
website: www.ncadd.org

NCADD is dedicated to fighting alcoholism, drug addiction, and the devastating consequences of alcohol and other drugs on individuals, families, and communities.

National Institute on Drug Abuse (NIDA)

6001 Executive Blvd.
Room 5213, MSC 9561
Bethesda, MD 20892
phone: (301) 443-1124
website: www.drugabuse.gov

NIDA supports and conducts research on drug abuse and aims to share that information in order to improve prevention and treatment of drug abuse and addiction.

Partnership for Drug-Free Kids

352 Park Ave. S., 9th Floor
New York, NY 10010
phone: (212) 922-1560 • fax: (212) 922-1570
website: www.drugfree.org

The goal of this nonprofit organization is to reduce substance abuse among adolescents and to help families impacted by addiction.

Substance Abuse and Mental Health Services Administration (SAMHSA)

1 Choke Cherry Rd.
Rockville, MD 20857
phone: (877) 726-4727
website: www.samhsa.gov

SAMHSA is the federal agency whose mission is to reduce the impact of substance abuse and mental illness on America's communities.

United Nations Office on Drugs and Crime (UNODC)

United Nations Headquarters
DC1 Building
Room 613
1 United Nations Plaza
New York, NY 10017
phone: (212) 963-5698 • fax: (212) 963-4185
website: www.unodc.org

The UNODC has offices all over the world working to fight illicit drugs, international crime, and terrorism.

US Drug Enforcement Administration (DEA)

8701 Morrissette Dr.
Springfield, VA 22152
phone: (202) 307-1000
website: www.dea.gov

The DEA is the federal agency that enforces controlled-substances laws and regulations. It also recommends and supports programs to reduce the availability of controlled substances.

FOR FURTHER RESEARCH

Books

Wayne Glausser, *Cultural Encyclopedia of LSD*. Jefferson, NC: McFarland, 2011.

Albert Hofmann, *LSD and the Divine Scientist: The Final Thoughts and Reflections of Albert Hofmann*. South Paris, ME: Park Street, 2013.

Cynthia Kuhn, Scott Swartzwelder, and Wilkie Wilson, *Buzzed: The Straight Facts About the Most Used and Abused Drugs from Alcohol to Ecstasy*. New York: Norton, 2014.

Peggy J. Parks, *Bath Salts and Other Synthetic Drugs*. San Diego, CA: ReferencePoint, 2014.

Thomas Santella, *Hallucinogens*. New York: Chelsea House, 2012.

Peter Stafford, *Psychedelics Encyclopedia*. Berkeley, CA: Ronin, 2013.

Internet Sources

Brian Alexander, "Return of Angel Dust? ERs See Spike in PCP, Synthetic Drugs," NBC News, December 3, 2013. www.nbcnews.com /health/health-news/return-angel-dust-ers-see-spike-pcp-synthetic -drugs-f2D11674428.

Benedict Carey, "LSD, Reconsidered for Therapy," *New York Times*, March 3, 2014. www.nytimes.com/2014/03/04/health/lsd-reconsid ered-for-therapy.html?_r=0.

Tia Ghose, "Magic Mushrooms Create a Hyperconnected Brain," LiveScience, October 29, 2014. www.livescience.com/48502-magic -mushrooms-change-brain-networks.html.

Melissa Healy, "First Trial of LSD as Medicine in 40 Years Shows Promise," *Los Angeles Times*, March 5, 2014. http://articles.latimes .com/2014/mar/05/science/la-sci-sn-lsd-trial-safety-20140304.

Stephanie O'Neill, "Psychedelic Science: The Surge in Psychiatric Re-search Using Hallucinogens," Southern California Public Radio, May 19, 2014. www.scpr.org/news/2014/05/19/44178/psychedelic-science-the-surge-in-psychiatric-resea.

Brooke S. Parish, "Hallucinogen Use," Medscape, November 23, 2015. http://emedicine.medscape.com/article/293752-overview.

INDEX

Note: Boldface page numbers indicate illustrations.

Abraham, Henry David, 24
addiction, 30–31
alkaloids, hallucinogenic, 6
Amend the RAVE Act campaign, 62
ayahuasca, 36
Ayers, Harry, 56–57

bad trips, 17–18, 34, 41, 42
Bassuk, Ellen L., 44
benzodiazepines, 46
Biden, Joe, 61
brain, 12, 25
  addiction and, 30
brain-blood barrier, 28

cannabinoids, 10
cannabis
  street names of, 7
  See also marijuana
Center for Behavioral Health
  Statistics and Quality, 51
Central Intelligence Agency (CIA),
  LSD and, 13
Clinton, Bill, 57
cognitive behavioral therapy
  (CBT), 50
Controlled Substances Act
  (1970), 14, 53

Dakwar, Elias, 38
Daly, Frank F., 17–18

DanceSafe, 59–60, 62
date-rape drugs, 61
dehydration, myth of, 27–29
dependence, psychological, 37
dissociative drugs, 19–20
Drug Abuse Resistance Education
  (D.A.R.E.) programs, 58, **59**
Drug Abuse Warning Network,
  41
Drummer, Olaf, 9

Earleywine, Mitch, 47
ecstasy. *see* methylenedioxymethamphetamine (MDMA)
electrolytes, 29
Elifson, Kirk W., 39–40
emergency room visits
  caregiver assessment of
    patients during, 42–44
  difficulty in diagnosis of drug
    taken, 46–48
  involving hallucinogen use, 41
Erowid (website), 19
Experience Project (website), 12

First, Michael B., 51
flashbacks, 23–25
Fuller, Crystal, 58

gateway drugs, 38–40
Gelenberg, Alan J., 44
Glick, Stanley, 36
Goldsmith, Dede, 62
Goldsmith, Shelley, 27–29, 62
Good Samaritan law, 64

Hales, Diana, 34–35
hallucinations, 7
hallucinogen persisting perception
    disorder (HPPD), 24–25
hallucinogens, 4
    addiction/dependence and,
        32–34
    banning of, 53
    classes of, 8–11
    dangers of combining, 28
    dental problems from, 21
    difficulty in identifying, in
        emergency situations, 46–48
    dissociative, 19–20
    effects of, 17–18
        short-term *vs.* long-term, **23**
    effects on personality/behavior,
        20–22
    in end-of-life care, 45
    first research on, 6–8
    as gateway drugs, 38–40
    in human history, 5
    legality of, 13–14
    percentage of teens never
        having tried, 54
    physical effects of, 25–26
    potential lifelong complications
        of, **35**, 39, 40
    prevalence of use, 14–15, **15**
    street names, 7
    as treatment for other drug
        addictions, 36
    as treatment for psychological
        disorders, 37–38
    workings of, 11–13
    See also prevention/prevention
        programs; treatment(s)
harm-reduction programs, 58–60
Hofmann, Albert, 6–7
hyperthermia, 26

ibogaine, 36
Illicit Drug Anti-Proliferation Act
    (2003), 61–62
indolealkylamines, 10–11

Journal of Neuroscience, 27
Jovi, Jon Bon, **63**
Joyner, Chuck, 22

Kamboukos, Dimitra, 14–15
Karch, Steven B., 9, 46
ketamine, 9
    dissociation and, 19–20
    street names of, 7
Kiyatkin, Eugene A., 28–29

Lewin, Louis, 6
Lewter, Mike, 42
Loflin, Mallory, 47
LSD. *See* lysergic acid
    diethylamide
lysergic acid diethylamide (LSD),
    6–8
    CIA's history with, 13
    street names of, 7
    as treatment for mood
        disorders, 37

marijuana, 9–10, **10**, 47
McKeever, Bridget Clare, 37
MDMA. *See* methylenedioxymeth-
    amphetamine
mescaline, 6, 11
methylenedioxymethamphetamine
    (MDMA), 11, **38**
    hyperthermia and, 26–27
    myth of dehydration from,
        27–29
    street names of, 7
    study of heaviest user of, 39

withdrawal symptoms from, 32
Mettes, Patrick, 45
Mitchell, Elizabeth, 26
MK-ULTRA project, 13
Morningside Recovery, 50
mushrooms
    street names of, 7
    see also indolealkylamines

National Institute on Drug Abuse
    (NIDA), 14, 53–54, 57–58
National Survey on Drug Use
    and Health (Substance Abuse
    and Mental Health Services
    Administration), 14, **15**
Native American Church, 57
neurotransmitters, 12, 22–23

Palamar, Joseph J., 14–15
PCP. *See* phencyclidine
peyote/peyote cacti, **5**, 5–6, 53
    legalization for religious use, 57
phencyclidine (PCP), 9
    dissociation and, 19–20
    signs of addiction to, **35**
    street names of, 7
    withdrawal symptoms from, 32
phenylethylamines, 11
piperidines, 8–9
plants, in human history, 4
post-traumatic stress disorder, 37
prevention/prevention programs,
    53–54
    evidence-based, 57–58
    harm-reduction approach *vs.*,
        58–59
    importance of teaching in
        schools/at home, 54–56
    role of parents in, 56–57
    setting realistic goals in, 64

Proposition 47 (CA), 61
Prytys, Cesia, 56–57
psilocybin, 45
psychedelic, origin of term, 17
Psychology Today (magazine),
    50

raves, 26, **27**
reality, dissociation from, 19–20
Reducing Americans' Vulnerability
    to Ecstasy (RAVE) Act (2003),
    61–62
Reid, Lesley W., 39–40
restraints
    chemical, 46
    physical, 44–46
rhabdomyolysis, 44–45
Rowe, Thomas C., 54–55
Rustin, Terry, 20

Sample, Lisa L., 58
Sanders, Lisa, 63
serotonin, 12
Sheff, David, 32–33
social inhibitions, 20
Späth, Ernst, 6
Stancliff, Sharon, 64
Steinorth, Marc, 61
Sterk, Claire E., 39–40
Strengthening Families Program,
    57
Substance Abuse and Mental
    Health Services Administration
    (SAMHSA), 14, 54
surveys, on hallucinogen use,
    14–15, **15**
Synovitz, Linda B., 55–56

Tasman, Allan, 51
tolerance, 34

Treatment Episode Data Set (Center for Behavioral Health Statistics and Quality), 51
treatment(s)
  of addiction, 30
  long-term, 48–50, 52
  of mood disorders, LSD as, 37
  for other drug addictions, hallucinogens as, 36
  for psychological disorders, hallucinogens as, 37–38, 47
  relapse following, 51

Underwood, Tyrone Lee, 21–22

violence, PCP and, 19–20, 22
Vletter, Dominique, 27–28

Wilson, C.W.M., 33, 34
Wood, Anna, 29
Wood, Ralph, 55–56
Wooldridge, Missi, 60

Yip, Luke, 17–18

PICTURE CREDITS

ABOUT THE AUTHOR

Jenny MacKay has written more than thirty books for teens and preteens on topics ranging from crime scene investigation and technological marvels to historical issues and the science of sports. She lives in Sparks, Nevada.